WE ARE G.U.™

The Origins, History, and Impact of Gonzaga University's Kennel Club™

Mike Shields & Aaron Hill

A KCOG Book

We Are G.U.: *The Origins, History, and Impact of Gonzaga University's Kennel Club*

Authors: Mike Shields and Aaron Hill

Copyright © 2018 KCOG, LLC

ISBN: 9780989035996
All Rights Reserved
Printed in the United States by Gray Dog Press,

For permissions and ordering information contact:
KCOG, LLC
6611 94th Street Ct NW
Gig Harbor, WA 98332
KCOGLLC@gmail.com

Book design: Jeffrey G. Dodd
Cover Image: Mike Wootton, courtesy of Gonzaga University Athletics.

DEDICATION

Dan Fitzgerald
March 3, 1942 – January 19, 2010

He put down the foundation for all of us. Without him, Mark [Few], Billy [Grier] and I would never have come to Gonzaga. When you talk about the 'Zag way,' the tradition, the Kennel Club, the way Gonzaga acts and plays, he was the foundation of all that. He was the cornerstone of Gonzaga basketball. He'll always be the founding father.

Dan Monson
Former Fitzgerald assistant and GU head coach
(1997-99)

There are the student sections you know: The Cameron Crazies at Duke; The Oakland Zoo at Pittsburgh; The Izzone at Michigan State. The Kennel Club, however, is a whole different animal.

Sports Capital Journalism Center/IUPUI.edu (2017)

CONTENTS

FOREWORD

You know the old notion: if people on all sides think you're wrong, you're probably doing something right.

This isn't a universal truth, of course, but in the case of the Kennel Club, it's pretty close.

Because when it comes to the KC, the darts come from all directions. Not that it's hate. Not at all. You can't be in the McCarthey Athletic Center on a big game night—Pepperdine or Santa Clara in the old days, Saint Mary's or BYU or anyone in the Top 25 of late—and hate what the Kennel Club brings to the vibe. College basketball is meant to be played in an atmosphere of both visual and visceral delights, and sometimes they have to be manufactured outside the lines.

The players can do their part: an alley-oop dunk, a get-that-outta-here blocked shot, an unconscionably deep 3-pointer that finds nothing but net as the Bulldogs break open another game.

But the rush from any of those plays is enhanced by the reaction of the eyewitnesses—roars that bow the walls, the animated delirium, the chants that tell the opponents they're down by 30 and the team bus is idling outside. And let's not forget getting in the visitors' heads in the warmups before tipoff.

At Gonzaga, this specifically is the job of the Kennel Club, the undergraduate parcel of the nightly sellout crowd that fills McCarthey's lower north side.

They're the ones in the synchronized shirts—or in the banana outfit, the bishop's mitre and the odd bathrobe.

On a given night, there might be a quartet of guys stripped to the waist, their chests lettered Z-A-G-S. They hoist the big-head portraits of the players, stomp and sway to Zombie Nation and clamor for the end-of-the-bench walk-ons to play when the game is out of hand.

By pretty much consensus acclaim—from the Zags players, assorted basketball meteorologists in the media and, yes, the members themselves—the KC is among the best at this particular craft in the country.

Is this a big deal?

Don't even bring up the KC's role in Gonzaga's glitzy home record since the McCarthey Athletic Center opened in 2004 (192-15; a cool 92.8 percent)—or that it was even better over the 12 years before that in the joint next door. Don't speculate how many times the KC's outsized presence clinched the deal on a recruit who made a visit on game night.

Just ask the opposing players and coaches who do their thing in home arenas that are half empty and often painfully indifferent.

So how did all of this begin and evolve?

Mike Shields and Aaron Hill are glad you asked. The two former Kennelmen have taken it upon themselves to detail the archeology of the KC, from the seed in 1984. That's right: it all got rolling back when Gonzaga basketball was just another game—those years when the KC itself never would have thought to make "Final Four" their flying-bodies spell-out during a timeout.

That's as much the phenomenon as the manic mob you see on ESPN game nights now.

It's a messy history, to be sure, and the authors acknowledge that the Kennel Club has never been everyone's cup of cheer.

Sedate fans across the gym thought the group unruly and coarse. The campus fathers blanched—at over-the-line language, over-imbibing at pre-funks and some overly entrepreneurial capitalism—and eventually brought the group under school control.

Which has only birthed different criticisms today. That the KC lacks creativity and danger. That the cheers are stale and the signs are lame. That the students only show up in full force for three or four big games.

Like we said, darts from all directions. Well, not all. You know who never complains?

The players.

Anyway, the point of the Kennel Club was never perfection. It was mostly to take something fun—Gonzaga basketball—

and make it more fun, and it seems as if the mission is still being accomplished.

Now take a walk through this history and see if it doesn't do the same thing.

John Blanchette

John Blanchette was Gonzaga basketball beat writer for The Spokesman-Review *from 1980-93, when he became the newspaper's full-time sports columnist. From his seat at the GU scorer's table, Blanchette witnessed the birth and evolution of the Kennel Club.*

INTRODUCTION

The Kennel Club is the embodiment of the Gonzaga spirit. The largest student group in the 130-year history of the University, it has become the most commonly shared experience among students and alumni. One cannot overstate the impact the Kennel Club has had on the University, its athletic programs and the student body, including student-athletes.

The story of the Kennel Club is in part the story of Gonzaga. It's the story of people, commitments, personal sacrifices and life-long friendships that are formed somewhere within the blurred line between adolescence and adulthood.

Gonzaga University is a special place. I recall people referring to "The Gonzaga Experience" as something one couldn't find anywhere else. After seven years on campus—five as an undergraduate and two pursuing a master's degree—my time at GU was among the best of my life, and friends I met at Gonzaga remain my best friends more than 35 years later.

One of my most memorable experiences at Gonzaga was being a part of the Kennel Club. It is astonishing to have seen the "club" grow from a small nucleus of students who supported a basketball program that had never been to a postseason tournament of any kind, to a group of nearly 2,000 members who regularly camp out in sub-freezing temperatures to secure a place to stand (not sit!) and watch a team that had made 19 straight NCAA tournament appearances leading up to competing in the national championship game in 2017.

Gonzaga's Kennedy Pavilion was opened in 1965, named in memory of President John F. Kennedy and featuring a dedication address from his brother, U.S. Senator Ted Kennedy. A 1986 donation to remodel the facility brought a name change. Until the basketball teams moved into the McCarthey Athletic Center in 2004, sold out crowds in The Charlotte Y. Martin Centre were often listed at 4,000, despite an actual capacity closer to 3,200.

How did this happen? How did a group of students coalesce around a program that had finished with a win-loss record of 13-14 the year prior to the genesis of the Kennel Club?

Before detailing the origins of the Kennel Club, it's important to note the groups and individuals who preceded it. Student support of Gonzaga basketball didn't begin with the KC. There were others. Notably, The Snake Pit.

According to Steve Robinson ('78), a Gonzaga alumnus who would eventually become the Chair of the GU Board of Regents, "Gonzaga's Snake Pit" was started during Adrian Buoncristiani's last season as the Bulldogs' head coach (1977-78). Members of the Snake Pit held pregame functions at Campus House and attended games in yellow T-shirts featuring a rattlesnake poised to strike.

As Paul Vogelheim ('77) tells it, the Snake Pit was named after a bar by the same name founded in 1880 in the mining and logging town of Enaville, Idaho. The bar, still open today, has a very colorful past, including once being a house of ill repute.

Although Gonzaga's Snake Pit was relatively small and had no organized chants or routines, they found other ways to make their presence known. One example is when the Zags played Big Sky Conference rival Montana in 1979; some Snake Pit members hosted a "John Stroeder Look-alike Contest" in honor of the Grizzlies' 6-foot 10-inch center. Stroeder—who later played in the NBA for the Milwaukee Bucks, Golden State Warriors and San Antonio Spurs—was mystified by the redheaded look-alikes standing along the sideline in front of the GU student section and was completely thrown off his game in the Zags' 56-52 win.

As a freshman in 1980-81, I partook in "halftime functions" at GU basketball games that involved upperclassmen dressed in Snake Pit T-shirts. Word would spread quickly through the student section that "refreshments" were being distributed from a keg in the back of a pick-up truck parked in the service alley that ran between Kennedy Pavilion and Pecarovich Field. A rock in the door on the east end of the gym allowed students to easily make their way between the festivities just outside the door and the game immediately inside.

Ken Devones ('77) recalls that prior to the time of the Snake Pit, GU students would jokingly misspell Coach Buoncristiani's name in spell-outs at Gonzaga basketball games:

"Give me a B!..."
"Give me an O!..."
"Give me a N!..."
"Give me a C!..."
"Give me a R!..."
"Give me an I!..."
"Give me a X!..."
"Give me a Y!..."
"What's that spell?"
"BUONCRISTIANI!"

Adrian Buoncristiani, Gonzaga men's basketball coach from 1972-78, had an overall record of 78–82 (.488).

Devones says that GU students of the mid-to-late 1970s were actually more active at baseball games than basketball games. Among their regular targets was Washington State's head baseball coach Frederick Charles Brayton, better known by his nickname "Bobo." He shared that name with a well-known gorilla at Seattle's Woodland Park Zoo. Taking that as their cue, Gonzaga students would greet the longtime WSU coach by throwing a banana— or sometimes small bunches of them—in his direction at games played at Pecarovich Field. Coach Brayton was always a good sport about it; I even remember times when he would pick up the bananas thrown at his feet, then peel and eat them while standing in the third base coach's box.

I also remember many late spring afternoons watching GU baseball games from the tree-lined hill above Pecarovich's third base/leftfield line where the shade from the evergreen trees kept beverages cold and out of sight, or an ice-filled hole in the hillside made a perfect resting spot for a keg. Those were the days when, if even a little discreet, a college student could enjoy a baseball game and a beer without much concern.

*When Mike Griffin ('82) donned his winged cap and cape, he transformed into
"Captain Zag," GU's human mascot before the official introduction of Spike the Bulldog.*

An example of individual student engagement at GU basketball games was "Captain Zag," a character created by Gonzaga student Mike Griffin ('82). He wore a winged cap and a cape branded with the letter "Z" and sometimes carried a mini-bullhorn. He was akin to a GU action hero who performed alongside the cheerleaders at all home games. Captain Zag was GU's human "mascot" before the costumed Spike the Bulldog. Griffin and the cheerleaders often performed on-the-floor spell-outs during timeouts. While this routine was similar to the ones performed by the Kennel Club just a few years later, Captain Zag's spell-out repertoire was much more limited, wasn't nearly as dynamic, and didn't result in as many on-court injuries as the high-flying KC version did.

Although there was an attempt to bring back Captain Zag after Mike Griffin graduated, it didn't really capture the imagination of the Gonzaga student body the second time around. Nothing against the young man who attempted to reprise the role, but it was a bit like when Roger Moore took over as James Bond after Sean Connery had become synonymous with the character. It

Gonzaga was a member of the Big Sky Conference from 1963 to 1979.

The West Coast Athletic Conference (WCAC) welcomed Gonzaga and the University of San Diego in 1979-80. A year later, Seattle University ended its participation at the Division I level, reducing the number of WCAC schools to eight.

The WCAC shortened its name to West Coast Conference (WCC) in 1989. Thirty years after its most recent expansion, BYU officially joined the West Coast Conference in 2011, followed by the return of University of the Pacific in 2013.

wasn't necessarily better or worse—it was just different seeing anyone other than Mike Griffin as Captain Zag.

Not a precursor to the Kennel Club, but an influencer, nonetheless, was the annual halftime show put on by the baseball team in the 1980s. This was done as a way to promote the opening of the GU baseball season and to introduce the team. The players would typically dress in full game uniforms, except spikes, of course, and perform a skit or funny routine at halftime of a men's basketball game, usually in late February.

One year they performed their standard baseball pre-game warmup, but without a ball and at about 3x speed. Watching them turn simulated double-plays and pointing out non-existent fly balls from their baseball positions on the basketball court was hilarious. In 1985, middle infielder Mike DeBenedetti led the team in a routine that included segments from the Bill Murray movie *Stripes* and music from the '70s TV show *Hawaii Five-O*.

ONE OF THE HIGHLIGHTS of this year's basketball season was the halftime show by the baseball team at the Pepperdine game.

The Gonzaga Bulletin
(1985)

So, for some of the younger members of the baseball team, seeing students with painted faces at games and coming out onto the floor to "perform" was all they had ever known. Thus, transitioning to the antics of the Kennel Club was easy—especially for the cast of characters on the team at that time.

While the students who founded and grew the Kennel Club were not the first GU students to rally behind the Zags, I believe the primary reason for the Kennel Club's longevity is that, unlike the Snake Pit, we had both upperclassmen and a very creative group of underclassmen—primarily GU baseball players—involved early on who passed along the traditions and created new ones.

Lastly, there has been talk of how the Kennel Club followed in the wake of the basketball program's success. Let me be clear: I don't claim that the KC led to the rise of the GU basketball program, but it certainly wasn't the other way around. The Kennel Club was founded in 1984. That was before GU had ever won a WCAC title; before the program had participated in a postseason tournament of any kind; before the Zags had played in a televised game beyond a local production; and before most of the college basketball world could even pronounce the word "Gonzaga."

Having said that, if you read the comments of the players and coaches in the pages that follow, it is clear that *they* believe that the Kennel Club changed the atmosphere at GU basketball games, and that change in the game environment, while not always comfortable for University administrators and some alumni, impacted the outcome of games, and in some cases the recruitment of players, in favor of the Zags.

Can I cite a specific event that triggered the creation of the Kennel Club? I've always been somewhat reluctant to answer that question by giving a specific "birth" event because—like the start of human life itself—there are people who fall on both sides of the conception/birth argument when it comes to the Kennel Club.

So I'll just give you my perspective, and let you decide.

Mike Shields ('84)

Mike Harrington ('84), left, and Mike Shields ('84).

*Otter: I think that this situation absolutely
requires a really futile and stupid
gesture be done on somebody's part!*

Bluto: We're just the guys to do it.

Animal House *(1978)*

CONCEPTION

In the fall of 1983, I moved into a University-owned house located at 624 East Sharp (where Goller Hall currently stands), across the street from the former grade school building which was then the home to the Gonzaga School of Law (where the Corkery Apartments are now located). My housemates were the same group I had shared a suite with in Cushing Hall during our junior year: Sean Hogan, Clay Simmons and Bob Twiss. Both Sean's and Bob's dads were GU graduates; Sean's dad served on Gonzaga's Board of Trustees, while Bob's dad was a member of the Board of Regents.

Our house on Sharp Avenue was located just steps from campus—behind Alliance House, an all-female dormitory. More importantly, the house was a half block down the alley from Pakies, a burger joint that doubled as our second home.

Our house rented for $275 per month (total!) and was situated between two other University houses. On one side lived a group of nuns in the Credo program, which attracted sisters from around the world to Gonzaga for their sabbatical studies, and on the other side lived a Dominican nun by the name of Sister Antonia who provided a home to a small group of young men with special needs.

Sister Antonia funded her mission by selling clothing and other household items that community members had donated to her. She kept most of the donated "inventory" stockpiled on the front porch of her house where she sold it daily and at larger events when she would display the items for sale on tables placed in her front yard. For that reason, my housemates and I lovingly referred to her as *Our Lady of the Perpetual Yard Sale.*

In addition to clothing and other household items, Sister Antonia also received donations of food from individuals, local grocery stores and bakeries to feed the young men in her care. To extend the life of those food donations, she had two large chest freezers whose precious contents were kept under lock and key, one inside the house and the other on her porch.

Earlier that fall, my parents, who still live in the Yakima Valley in Eastern Washington, purchased a side of beef from a local rancher. When I came home for Thanksgiving, they gave me a large box of wrapped meats to take back to school with me. However, the small refrigerator freezer in our Gonzaga house (which hadn't been defrosted since the day we moved in) had barely enough space for a couple of ice cube trays, let alone a box full of beef.

Knowing that Sister Antonia had not one, but two chest freezers at her disposal, I thought I would ask if she would allow me to store the meat in one of them and take portions out as needed. As I approached her door with the box in hand, Sister Antonia rushed out of her house and greeted me at her doorstep. I could see that she had immediately noticed the box I was holding, but before I had a chance to explain, she clasped her hands over her heart and with tears in her eyes said, "Oh, Michael! God bless you! This will feed my boys for weeks!"

I didn't have the heart to tell her I wasn't intending to give her the box of steaks, roasts and other cuts of meat, but truth be told it ended up in the right place; she needed it much more than my housemates and I did. So I just played along as if I was a generous benefactor and helped her load her newly-donated treasure into her freezers. Although it dramatically altered the "meal plan" at our house for the remainder of the semester, the owners of Pakies were grateful for our continued patronage, I'm sure.

The sisters on both sides of us were incredibly kind. Not only did they tolerate our constant noise violations and parties, but it also wasn't unusual for us to go out to pick up the Sunday morning newspaper after a late night of partying and find a gallon of milk and a dozen donuts waiting for us outside our front door.

The sports section of the newspaper was always the first taken. All of us were huge sports fans. We had all played various sports in high school and we all played together on intramural teams in every sport at Gonzaga. We were also intensely loyal fans of the men's basketball team. In my undergraduate years at GU, I don't believe I missed a single home game while school was in session, including the occasional game or tournament at the old Spokane Coliseum. In fact, Bob Twiss and I attended the Far West Classic in Portland that was played in the midst of one of the Rose City's legendary ice storms. Many consider that tournament as our classmate John Stockton's coming-out party—he was named tournament MVP after the Zags beat Robert Morris University; lost to tournament co-host Oregon, led by future NBA center Blair Rasmussen; and collected a rare win (at least at that time) over Washington State to take third place.

Late in that season (1983-84), the Zags played Whitworth College at GU. It was one of those mid-week, out-of-conference games that WCAC teams played to fill a hole in the schedule during the same week they played their league travel partner—in Gonzaga's case, it was their longtime rival: The University of Portland.

My brother Tim, who was a freshman at the time, was sitting behind me at the game. During a timeout, the Whitworth cheerleaders took the floor and performed a routine ot impressive acrobatic flips and lifts in front of a partisan, albeit subdued, Gonzaga crowd. At the end of their routine, the Whitworth cheer squad left the floor to complete and utter silence; not a single clap of the hands could be heard from the crowd in Kennedy Pavilion, GU's slightly larger than high-school-sized gym.

At that point Tim tapped me on the shoulder and said, "Let's go out there!" I don't know what prompted him to want to do that, but Tim and I had each been class clowns in high school, so it wasn't all that unusual for us to try to make people laugh—although neither of us had ever attempted to do so in such a public way.

We were certainly taking the risk of receiving the same crowd reaction as the Whitworth cheer squad had just received or, worse still, getting kicked out of the building for coming onto the floor during a game, but the timeout was ending and I didn't have time to think, so I just bounded down a couple of rows from my bleacher seat in the student section, and dove onto the floor around mid-court.

Tim followed close behind and hopped over me a couple of times, and then we both began jumping around in an attempt to show the fans in attendance that GU had some acrobats, too! As the timeout buzzer sounded and both teams began heading back onto the court, Tim and I went running back to our seats to some applause, and a lot of laughter.

Our friend Scott Bauer captured that moment in a photo that still hangs on my office wall. In that instant, Scott became our unofficial, official photographer.

As we were making our way out of the gym after the game, several administrators and alumni approached me to say what a kick they got out of our "routine." I remember thinking that instead of getting in trouble, we were getting positive reinforcement!

But the week following our "performance," I got a call from Wilma Brickner, ticket manager and secretary for Gonzaga's Athletic Director Dan Fitzgerald—who everyone, from Jesuit priests to students like me, referred to as "Fitz." I had worked in and around the GU Athletics department my entire four years at the school. Still, I was a bit surprised to get a call at home from Fitz's secretary asking me to meet with him.

So, as requested, I went down to Fitz's office in Kennedy Pavilion and waited. As I sat in a chair outside his office I thought,

"The jig is up." I was sure that I was about to have a "Come to Jesus" meeting with a guy who could be a bit intimidating when he wanted to be. Fitz had a well-deserved reputation for being fiery; there was a reason why longtime GU radio broadcaster Dick Wright regularly described him as "The Mad Irishman stomping the sidelines" after a bad call by the referees.

Suddenly, his office door swung open. Fitz stuck his head out, looked at me and said, "Come on in." As I walked past him he closed the door behind me and said, "Sit down." By this time my heart was pounding in my chest. He began by saying he had noticed that my friends and I came to every game; I nodded. I was sure the next words out of his mouth were going to question why I thought it was okay for a student to come out of the stands and run onto the floor during a game. But to my great relief, he said that he liked what we did and wanted us to keep it up. He then leaned across his desk, looked me square in the eyes and said, "Make sure you make it to the game tonight."

With that, I went running back to our house on Sharp Avenue and told my housemates about my "meeting" with Fitz. We had been given a mission; we had to act fast. We had to promote and execute a pregame party on short notice. We wanted to show a unified front, so we made the quick decision that we wouldn't charge anyone to come to the party as long as they painted their face and went to the game to cheer with us... It's amazing what college students will do in exchange for free beer!

There were around 50 students who came to that first party, painted their faces and went to the game. As I recall, we pretty much stayed in the stands, but we were LOUD! In the few remaining home games after that, we became more and

Left to right: Bob Twiss, Mike Shields, Tim Neuen-schwander, Joe Roberts and John Grant.

(Note: Jack & Clemy Stockton standing just below the rail in Section E. This was John Stockton's senior season, and the Stockton's were at every home game, just as they had been since his freshman year.)

15

more bold—going out on the court almost immediately became commonplace. After only a couple of games, the GU cheerleaders began asking us for permission to go out onto the floor during a timeout. Often the answer was "No, we have something planned" (which, of course, we didn't).

Nothing beyond getting the entire crowd involved in chants of "G-U" and "Bull-dogs" were planned more than a couple of minutes in advance. Our most creative stuff came out during the flow of the game. There was a game that took place during a break when many of the students had returned home. The opponent was the standard NAIA or Division II team, typically from Montana, Idaho or Eastern Oregon, or wherever Fitz could pull them in from for a single game in Spokane. Anyway, "Team X" had a 7-footer who had a bit of a Neanderthal look to him. Bob Twiss took one look at him and said, "He looks like Herman Munster!" So now we had a gym with maybe 1,000 people in it chanting, "Her-man Mun-ster! Her-man Mun-ster!" every time the poor guy touched the ball.

We got so used to doing whatever we wanted that we would actually take the cheerleaders' megaphones and use them to yell at players, coaches and the referees. The refs were so caught off guard by our antics that they didn't quite know what to do. There were times when opposing players would be taking the ball out of bounds in front of the student section, and they would be virtually surrounded by guys with painted faces who were screaming directly into their ears. The referees seemed oblivious to it—I don't recall a single time when we were told to back off.

Unintentionally, I'm sure, the school added fuel to the fire when they gave away kazoos at that season's homecoming game.

Left to right: Pete Erie, Joe Roberts, Sean Hogan, Jim Hilger and Bob Twiss lead the crowd in a chant during a timeout in the 1983-84 season.

Note: Fr. Tony Lehmann, SJ, seated at the end of the GU bench at the far left.

At halftime, we all played along and formed what was billed as "the world's largest kazoo band." After a short while, some of the guys got bored with it and decided to break out on their own—Jon Bolling and Joe Roberts ran onto the court to dunk their kazoos through the hoop, and suddenly, the entire student section showered the floor with kazoos. While the players waited to take the floor for the second half, the game staff swept hundreds of kazoos into a pile using a push broom.

In the 1980s and into the '90s fans could walk up to the Kennedy Pavilion/Martin Centre doors without a game ticket and find a great seat. However, if you look at the pictures from that era, including those on the pages here, you will notice very few, if any, empty seats. As much as I'd like to give the Kennel Club credit for increasing fan support, I have to give credit where credit is due— and in the case of the 1983-84 season, it was due largely to John Stockton.

John was (is) the epitome of a hometown hero. He grew up in the "Little Vatican" neighborhood of Spokane which includes the GU campus; he went to St. Aloysius Grade School and Gonzaga Prep; his grandfather was a legendary Gonzaga football player; and his father, Jack Stockton, co-owned and operated Jack & Dan's Tavern which—along with what was then The Bulldog Tavern—was (is) a Gonzaga hang-out. Many Stockton family friends and people in the community who had known John growing up regularly attended GU games.

John had a great senior season. He was named WCAC Player of the Year and an Academic All-American. He was invited to the Olympic try-out camp at Indiana University that summer, and was one of Olympic coach Bobby Knight's final cuts. He was selected in the first round of the 1984 NBA Draft by the Utah Jazz. That draft class—which included Hakeem Olajuwon, Michael Jordan and Charles Barkley—is widely considered the NBA's best ever.

But even with a player who many consider the greatest pure point guard in the history of the game, the Zags finished fourth in the WCAC with a 17-11 record. In the days before a conference tournament and automatic bid into the NCAA Tournament, and before the "Big Dance" expanded to 64 teams in 1985, a 17-win season was far from good enough for a fourth place WCAC team to get a postseason invite, even from the then-relevant National Invitation Tournament (NIT). So Stockton's collegiate career ended just as the Kennel Club's run was about to begin.

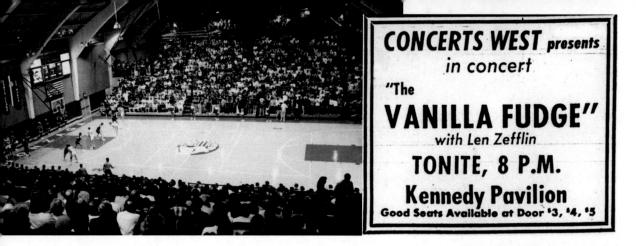

Above: In addition to being the home for several GU athletic teams, Kennedy Pavilion hosted events throughout the '60s and '70s. A 1968 Vanilla Fudge concert listed opening act "Len Zefflin." A bootleg recording of the show was the first-ever live recording of a Led Zeppelin performance.

Right: Charlie Vogelheim's ('78) original Snake Pit shirt. The Snake Pit, a popular precursor to today's Kennel Club, was named after a 135-year-old bar in Enaville, Idaho.

Dominican Sister Antonia Stare died Dec. 24, 2012.

According to The Inland Register, she became a member of the Dominican Sisters in 1934.

Sister Antonia served as a nursing supervisor in Tonasket, Washington, and then as a teacher in several locations in central and eastern Washington.

The Register adds that she was "director of Starry Home, Spokane, from 1978-1994. She then began ministry as a parish visitor for St. Aloysius Parish, Spokane, until 2006, followed by life in community at St. Joseph Care Center, Spokane, until her death."

We didn't really know what we were doing when Fitz and Coach Hertz approached us about naming our group of rowdies. Nor did we really know that few schools in 1984—particularly those with relatively little basketball history, like Gonzaga—had a named student section. For example, the official webpage of college basketball's most famous student section, Duke's Cameron Crazies, states the group was founded "sometime in the mid-80s;" another site states the first official use of the name was in 1986. My housemate Joe Roberts suggested the name "Kennel Club," so with Dale Goodwin's help I set off making our first shirt, which turned out to be an immediate hit.

The original
Kennel Club shirt

By the time Stockton was a senior, Fitzgerald figured he needed to do something to stoke student attendance. And thus was born the Kennel Club, the band of student rowdies who heat the gym to sweaty levels and make life regrettable for opposing players.

Seattle Times *(2004)*

BIRTH

The 1984-85 academic year was my fifth year at GU, or as some call it, my "victory lap." I had switched majors midway through my sophomore year and needed only 12 more credits to graduate with a degree in Economics. Rather than taking my four remaining classes during the fall semester and graduating in December, I decided to spread those credits over two semesters so that I only had classes on Tuesdays and Thursdays. I waited tables a few days a week at The Old Spaghetti Factory in downtown Spokane; otherwise, I had time on my hands.

One of the things I did to fill my time was serving as the student manager of the Gonzaga baseball team. I had been the manager the year before, too, so I knew the players well. The baseball players came to every basketball game, but they weren't a part of the "painted face crew."

The great thing about the baseball players was that trash-talking or "ragging" seemed to come naturally to them. And GU had some of the best "raggers" around— sophomores Chris McGahan, Tim O'Neil, Jeff Zenier and freshman Jeff Cummins were creative and funny, and senior Mike DeBenedetti had a very quick wit and a great sense of humor. More importantly, they were somehow capable of researching the backgrounds of opposing players long before the public had access to computers, let alone the internet or social media.

I later found out that they were regular visitors to Dale Goodwin's office. As Sports Information Director, Dale had access to all the opposing teams' media guides and press releases. Those guys took what little information they could glean from those publications and coupled it with their creativity to produce some hilarious comments and chants that caught the attention of the opposing team's players—usually during warmups when they would be within easy earshot.

Regardless of the source of their information, those guys were amazing in the level of detail they obtained. Joining forces with the baseball team really elevated our "game."

Before the start of the conference basketball season, Fitz asked to meet with a group of us at our house on East Baldwin Avenue. The group included two of my new housemates, Mike Harrington and Joe Roberts, as well as GU baseball players Chris McGahan and Tim O'Neil. Fitz brought with him men's basketball assistant coach Joe Hillock, Sports Information Director Dale Goodwin, and head baseball coach Steve Hertz.

The purpose of the meeting was, it seemed, to corral this group of wild mustangs as well as to brand them. On the surface, the corralling part must have seemed simple—with coach Hertz involved the baseball team would fall in line (well, somewhat). Now we just needed a brand. We discussed several name options, including "The Dog House" and "The Dog Pound," but when Joe Roberts said, "How about the Kennel Club?" we all knew we had a winner.

Joe recently told me that he suggested that name because he thought that "The Dog Pound" meant mutts whereas the "Kennel Club" suggested sophistication and good breeding. I'm not sure anything we said or did suggested sophistication and good breeding, but I think the name is perfect for a group supporting the Bulldogs!

Once we had a name, we needed something to make us identifiable as a group. I designed the first Kennel Club shirts utilizing a logo that Dale Goodwin had created a few years earlier. I sketched out how the shirt would look and posted a sign-up sheet on our refrigerator prior to a pregame party. By the end of the night, every line of the order sheet was filled.

The first run of 30 shirts cost me $3 each to produce; I sold them for $8. Once students saw the shirts, they became so popular that I produced a second run and began sending them to the alums who had been a part of the original "painted face crew." I used the profits from the sale of the shirts to pay my rent for a couple of months—it was better than waiting tables!

Now that we were somewhat legitimate—with an official name and club shirts—we hit the ground running, literally. We had started coming out on the floor during GU player introductions the year before, but it was during this time that forming a tunnel became a regular occurrence. Many students, led by the Kennel Clubbers, would come pouring out of the stands to create a tunnel for the Zags to run through as they were introduced.

All-WCAC player Bryce McPhee, who was in his fifth year after suffering a serious leg injury the year before, described the scene like this: "During the announcement of the starting lineups, students would completely ignore the other team and then, unheard of at the time, storm the court creating a giant tunnel. The starters would weave through the tunnel and the place would go absolutely crazy."

The Kennel Club's first on-court routine may have been the acrobatic, human spell-out. The individual participants might have changed a bit from game to game, but it was primarily the baseball players who dove around on the floor to form each letter in the word "ZAGS" or, if we were really ambitious, "GONZAGA." It was hilarious to watch as they would jump over each other to get into the right formation, which wasn't always easy to do under the circumstances (if you know what I mean).

> # I COULDN'T WAIT for my first start and the experience of running through the Kennel Club tunnel. It was even better than I dreamed it would be.
>
> Mike Nilson
> 2000 WCC
> Defensive Player
> of the Year

We also became quite adept at identifying the player or players on the opposing team whom we would pick on throughout the game. Jeff Zenier was particularly good at noticing players who were taking note of what we were saying to them—or "rabbits" as Zenier and the baseball players called them on account of their use of their "big ears" to listen and react to everything that was being said. We would often pick out a rabbit during warmups and begin booing every time he would touch the ball. This continued into the game where we would boo every time that player had the ball, and for as long as he held onto it. As soon as he would pass or shoot, we would stop booing.

McGahan, O'Neil, Cummins and Shane McClary all went to Crespi Carmelite, a Catholic, all-male college prep school in Encino, California. There were a number of other GU baseball players also from Southern California, the Bay Area, Portland and

Seattle, so it was often the case one of them would know some tidbit of information that we could use against opposing players from their home area.

One example was Greg Goorjian. He was a Southern California high school basketball legend. He averaged over 40 points per game his senior year at Crescenta Valley High School, where his dad, Ed, was head coach. Greg Goorjian initially played for Arizona State, and then transferred to the University of Nevada at Las Vegas (UNLV); his senior year he transferred to Loyola Marymount University (LMU) to play for his dad, who by that time was the head coach of the Lions.

Two years earlier, we had derided the younger Goorjian with chants of "Daddy's boy! Daddy's boy!" every time he touched the ball, which was a LOT, because he led the WCAC in scoring with over 26 points per game.

But now we were the Kennel Club! The bar had been raised; we had to come up with something more creative for Ed Goorjian's return to Gonzaga.

Coach Goorjian had dark, thick, curly hair perched atop his head. In those days it could have been a perm, or just naturally curly, but to a group of college-age guys looking for anything we could exploit, it didn't look real. So during an early timeout in the LMU game, the Kennel Club did a spell-out of the word "TOUPEE" at mid-court. The entire building erupted in laughter as soon as they realized what we were spelling (it's a miracle we spelled it right, or maybe we didn't, and that's why they were laughing).

Sometime in the second half, I noticed that Coach Goorjian started pointing in our direction from the LMU bench. He would grab an assistant coach or a nearby player, and angrily say something to them while pointing at us in the student section. At the end of the game, he calmly shook the hands of the Gonzaga coaches and players and then came storming across the court toward us—I truly thought he was coming to take us all on! Instead, he called us all together and said, "I wish we had guys like you at LMU."

I think that was a widely-held sentiment among opposing coaches. As much as we may have annoyed them, disrupted their team, or influenced the officials, they were envious of the home court advantage we had given the Zags. GU head coach Jay Hillock told me at the time that he believed that the Kennel Club was worth 6-8 points per game to his team.

The moment I first realized the direct impact the Kennel Club could have on a game was when Santa Clara visited Kennedy

Pavilion in 1985. The Broncos had a 7-foot 1-inch all-conference center by the name of Nick Vanos. Vanos averaged more than 12 points and almost eight rebounds per game over the course of his career at SCU (1981-85), but he wasn't a particularly good free throw shooter, averaging less than 60% over that same timespan.

Given his height, there was an ever-so-slight resemblance between Vanos and Lurch, the giant butler on *The Addams Family* TV show. Again, "ever-so-slight" was ever-so-good-enough for the Kennel Club.

So, when Vanos reached the free throw line for the first time, the entire Kennel Club began to "sing" the intro to *The Addams Family* theme song (You know, *Na-na Na-na, snap...snap...*). As the referee handed Vanos the ball to shoot his free throws, the Santa Clara bench realized what we were doing and they all began to laugh. Then Vanos started laughing, so much so that he had to step away from the free throw line to compose himself. I don't recall if he made the free throws or not, but just knowing that we could influence the play of the opposing team in that way caused us to want to do it more.

> # THE KENNEL CLUB
> ## is the best thing that has happened to Gonzaga basketball since I've been here.
>
> ### Jay Hillock
> Head Coach 1981-85
> *The Gonzaga Bulletin*
> (1985)

Even though the Kennel Club was merciless when his LMU Lions came to Gonzaga, coach Ed Goorjian (left) couldn't help but respect their passion and devotion.

THE HOUSE(S) THE KENNEL CLUB BUILT

Without a doubt, house parties were a big part of the growth of the Kennel Club. Those parties broke down any barriers between the core group of Kennel Clubbers and the rest of the student body. The parties also made it possible for underclassmen who didn't know any of the older KC members or baseball players to become engaged in the group.

In 1984-85, I lived in a house a few blocks north of campus on East Baldwin with Mike Harrington, Joe Roberts, Tony Rose, Clay Simmons and an Eastern Washington University student named Vince Cubbage. Joe and Vince both just happened to work at Fitz's favorite restaurant and postgame hang-out, Chapter Eleven, and I worked with Vince's sister at the Old Spaghetti Factory. Our house and "The Baseball House" on Mission were the sites of Kennel Club parties during the basketball season, and house parties alternating every other weekend the remainder of the year.

The guys who lived at The Baseball House were players Chris McGahan, Tim O'Neil, Gregg Harris and Kevin Toliver, along with their friends Bill Slattery and John Webber. We had an arrangement where they could get into our parties for free, and we could do the same at their place.

Gonzaga first baseman/designated hitter Jeff Hainline was the "doorman" at most of our parties on East Baldwin. The Hainline name is legendary within Gonzaga's baseball program. Jeff's older brother, Bill, was an all-conference shortstop on a GU baseball team that advanced to the NCAA regional finals—one step shy of the College World Series—before getting beat by national powerhouse Arizona State. The Zags were ranked 11th in the nation after the 1978 season and 9th in the 1980 postseason poll.

To say Jeff Hainline was a power hitter would be an understatement. He hit 21 home runs his freshman season (1984)—a record for the then-Pac-10 North—and he hit 54 HRs in his Gonzaga career, a number that tied him for the all-time Pacific-10 Conference record with USC's Mark McGwire.

The other baseball player who played a role at our house parties was outfielder Jeff Zenier. We weren't sophisticated enough to have a deejay at our parties, but Zenier, who still goes by the nickname "7," always seemed to gravitate toward coordinating the music. While most of my housemates and I were die-hard Bruce Springsteen fans, "Z" realized that *Darkness on the Edge of Town* wasn't exactly what most co-eds preferred to listen to at house parties. "Z" has eclectic musical tastes running from heavy metal to hip-hop, but he always found the sweet spot by getting into the mix a few Jackson Five hits and dance favorites like "ABC" and "I Want You Back."

Regardless of the type of music that was played, those parties were usually blow-outs. On one occasion, we painted The Wall next to Crosby Library to promote a party at our house featuring "15 Barrels of Barley Pop." We had kegs flowing non-stop; one in our kitchen and two in our basement. Over the course of the night, we must have had 400-500 people in our house.

The Baldwin House had a deck and an above-ground pool in the backyard. Eventually, people started jumping off the deck into the pool, and there were even a few "ambitious" partiers who thought they might jump off our roof into the water (they didn't). By the end of the night, every piece of deck furniture we had could be found at the bottom of the pool. We thought that epic party would never be topped, but The Baseball House managed to go through 16 kegs the following weekend.

I have told this story many times, and I'm not sure the people I've told it to have always believed me, but it's the God's honest truth:

Throughout that year, we would toss the tap covers off the top of the kegs into a drawer in our kitchen; I don't know why, maybe

25

for the same reason empty beer bottle collections can be found in the dorm room of virtually every college-aged male in America. As we were moving out of The Baldwin House at the end of the school year, I decided to count the tap covers. There were well over one hundred in that drawer, and I'm sure The Baseball House went through a number close to that.

Taking into account Thanksgiving break, Christmas break and spring break, there are about 25-30 weekends in the academic year when students are on campus (basically Labor Day through Mother's Day). You do the math; it makes my head hurt just thinking about it.

Kennel Club kindles craziness

Kennedy Pavilion, alias the Doghouse, has always been a dreaded stop for Gonzaga's opponents. But this year Kennedy Pavilion has become an even more intimidating place for opponents to visit.

One of the main reasons for this is Gonzaga's rowdy bunch of fans that call themselves the Kennel Club. The Kennel Club is led by Mike Sheilds and the baseball team, who do everything from chant at opposing players to lead cheers during timeouts.

"The Kennel Club is the best thing that has happened to Gonzaga basketball since I've been here," said Gonzaga head coach Jay Hillock. "They create a lot of interest and enthusiasm in the other students."

Unlike many college gyms, where the student body section is located in the upper balcony region, Gonzaga's student body section is right next to the court. This allows the Kennel Club to get right into the action.

"The Kennel Club, the Pep Squad and the rest of the student body give us the biggest home court advantage in our conference. Nobody else has a crowd quite like ours. Others are not as cruel and vociferous," Hillock said.

Since Kennedy Pavilion opened in 1965 the Zaga have run up a home court record of 175-69. Over the last 6½ years they have won 64 of 85 games. So far this year the Zags are 10-1 at home with the only loss coming to Santa Clara in overtime.

"They (the Kennel Club) are crazy with class," said Hillock. "We are happy for their support. It makes it difficult for teams to play here. I hope it is an ongoing thing."

Tim Ruff, a senior Bulldog said: "It's really nice to see the fans get into the game. No one in our conference has a crowd like we do."

SCOTT BAUER

Mike Shields and the Kennel Club lead a cheer at a recent game.

The January 31, 1985, issue of The Gonzaga Bulletin *includes coach Joe Hillock's acknowledgement of the club's value to the team.*

BASEBALL TAKES THE LEAD

I got to know baseball player Tim O'Neil ("Onie," "T.O." or simply "O" as he was known) during his freshman year at GU (1983-84). Tim told me that the team didn't have a student manager and asked if I would be interested. After working on the basketball clean-up crew the previous few years, switching over to the baseball team seemed like it could be fun. So Tim introduced me to head coach Steve Hertz, who offered me a work-study job that entailed helping with the field set-up for practices and games, as well as working with trainer Steve DeLong on caring for the uniforms and other equipment.

I didn't realize how little I knew about the game until I began spending every day around the team. But by the middle of the season, I had gained the trust of the coaches to the point that they asked me to relay signals from the dugout during games. The system was simple: Coach Hertz would quietly tell me what he wanted the hitter or baserunner to do, and I would relay that information from the dugout to those players by subtly touching the bill of my cap, crossing my arms, or some other motion or stance. To this day, when I run into some of the players from that team, they will invariably ask me to remind them of the "take" or "hit-and-run" sign. But having that responsibility wasn't without its consequences.

We were on our spring trip in 1984 when we played UCLA in Westwood. I was a bit in awe being at Jackie

Opened in 1967, Pecarovich Field sat where the McCarthey Athletic Center now stands. The field was named after former Gonzaga athlete and coach Mike Pecarovich. The stadium was later renamed August/A.R.T. Stadium after former Gonzaga coach and benefactor Joey August and the Athletic Round Table, a club of sports boosters started in 1920. In 2007, the inaugural game was played at Gonzaga's new baseball facility: Patterson Baseball Complex/ Washington Trust Field.

The Hill Crew comprised a few men's basketball players and their friends who attended GU baseball games to support the team.

The group's name refers to the hill that ran along the third base/left field line at Pecarovich Field.

The "crew" would often put a keg in the back of a pick-up truck and park it on Cincinnati Street (across from St. Catherine/St. Monica Hall) so they could watch the game while having a few beers.

In addition to ragging the opposing team, they sometimes entered the field between innings to perform The Wave or some other routine.

1988 Gonzaga Baseball Staff
Left to right, Kneeling: Dale Goodwin (Sports Information Director), Steve Hertz (14); Standing: Steve DeLong (Trainer), Tim O'Neil (6), Chris Spring (30), Mark Machtolf (27), Mike Shields (Graduate Assistant).

On May 11, 2018, the baseball field was re-dedicated to become Patterson Baseball Complex/Coach Steve Hertz Field presented by Washington Trust. Hertz served 24 years as head baseball coach and is the University's winningest coach.

Gonzaga baseball pitcher Chris "Magic" McGahan created havoc at basketball games with his "Rah" seat and sporting a signature houndstooth jacket and orange Chuck Taylor's. At "No Refs" nights, he spared the refs no mercy while wearing a custom-made striped bag on his head.

Above: The calm before the storm. First row, left to right: John Webber, Joel Marx, Tim O'Neil, Mike Shields, Mike DeBenedetti, Ron Davis, Danny Morris, Pat Mulligan, Vince Cubbage. Second row: Tim Shields, two unidentified, Joe Roberts, Steve Suarez, unidentified woman, Reed Armijo, Jeff Hainline. Third row: Chris Spring, Tom Bennett, Dan Beach, Dave Rainey. Fourth row: Clete Wise.

Left: Left to right: Steve Hertz, Steve DeLong, Dan Fitzgerald during Gonzaga baseball's trip to the Soviet Union in June 1989.

Robinson Stadium and seeing future major leaguers like the Bruins' Shane Mack play. About midway through the game, GU finally had a runner advance to third base. Coach Hertz walked by me and said, "Be ready to put on the squeeze (bunt)." As I stood on the dugout steps next to pitcher Chris McGahan, I prepared myself to relay the sign which would require me to squat down. After a few pitches, the count was such that Coach Hertz decided not to go forward with the squeeze play. He walked behind me and quietly said, "Forget it." I didn't hear what he said so I turned to Chris who told me Hertzie had said, "Go for it." Not having the time to confirm with Coach Hertz, and not wanting to call any attention to myself that would give the play away, I gave the squeeze sign and the batter laid down a bunt; the Bruins cleanly fielded the ball and threw the runner out at home. Hertzie spun around and looked at me as if to say, "WTH!" In the time it took for me to look back toward Chris, he had slipped away and found a seat at the other end of the dugout! I was alone on an island; I felt terrible after having ended the GU scoring threat. Luckily for me, my mistake wasn't the difference as the Bruins won the game easily.

Despite the occasional hiccup, I really enjoyed being around the guys on the team. I learned a lot about "ragging" from some of the best around, McGahan among them.

One of the many things I learned being around the team was the creative language of the game. I remember Jeff Zenier saying a player had "Madlocked" it into second base, in reference to major leaguer Bill Madlock's tendency to nonchalantly step on the bag to narrowly beat a throw rather than to slide safely. Terms and phrases like "through the five hole" (a ground ball that goes between the fielder's legs), describing a batter as a "Punch and Judy hitter" (a spray hitter with little or no power) or shouting "boot it!" just as an opposing player was fielding a ground ball were all commonplace. I laughed harder than everyone else, mainly because I had never heard banter like that between those on the field of play and those off it. That is one of the reasons the GU baseball team was so integral to the growth and development of the Kennel Club —they knew how to "rag" and were completely uninhibited in interacting with players on the court before or even during games. Maybe some of their ragging abilities came about because they had been the targets of it themselves.

The following season (1984-85), I again went on the then-annual spring break trip with the team to Southern California. While a week-long stay in sunny Southern California certainly was enticing for a group of 18-22 year olds recovering from a long, cold Spokane winter, we dreaded the 24-hour bus ride it took to get there. That year, we rode directly from Spokane to the Pepperdine campus in Malibu, California, where the players stepped straight off the bus for a day-before-the-game practice.

By the time spring break rolled around, the Zags may have played three or four games, *IF* Pecarovich Field had thawed. Meanwhile, the Waves and other Southern California-based teams may have had 15-20 games under their belts. The highly-ranked Pepperdine baseball team was already in mid-season form, and their fans were too.

Remember, this was the baseball season after the Kennel Club had been formed. The Pepperdine basketball team had experienced the wrath of the Kennel Club (which they knew was mainly GU baseball players) during the basketball season, and they came prepared for revenge. A group of Pepperdine students, including basketball players, sat directly behind home plate and brought with them blocks of wood that, when slapped together, created a deafening sound. And when they weren't creating that kind of noise, they were talking some serious noise.

For instance, they told Jeff Hainline, who they dubbed "Waistline," that if he got a hit there would be a jelly donut waiting for him at first base. And when he struck out, they offered to put the donuts in the dugout for him instead. When catcher Scott Burkhardt hit a home run, they sang "Happy Birthday" to him as he rounded the bases. In between, they had clever comments for every batter as he stepped to the plate and throughout his entire at-bat. It was then the GU baseball players knew they had to step up their "game" as well.

The next basketball season, the baseball team instituted a few new Kennel Club routines. One example was The "Rah" Seat. Gonzaga assistant basketball coach Joe Hillock had introduced Chris McGahan to the idea. Outfielder Tom Bennett took a toilet seat and painted the lid blue and the seat red, and on the inside of the lid he painted the word "Rah."

During a timeout, Chris would run to the middle of the court and show the seat to both sides of the gym. He would then open up the seat and close it. Every time he opened the seat showing the word "Rah" inside the lid, the crowd would yell out "Rah!" for as long as he had it opened. He would then close it and the crowd would go silent. He would go to the student side and open it up; then he would go to the season ticketholder side and do the same thing. He would sometimes chase a referee around the court opening and closing the lid so fast that the crowd's repeated and rapid-fire "Rahs" had the effect of a dog barking at the ref.

Only Chris could have gotten away with that, and he was perfect for this role; he was (is) quite a character. He was the most gregarious guy on campus. He knew and was friends with EVERYONE.

Chris was on the floor a lot at games. So much so that he developed a bit of an on-court persona. He began to wear a houndstooth jacket over his Kennel Club shirt, and a pair of orange Converse Chuck Taylor high tops rounded out his game-day wardrobe.

Chris became the embodiment of the Kennel Club. He was even chosen to "box" GU mascot Spike the Bulldog (Lee Mauney '88) during the halftime of one of the games. The University used footage of the "fight" to produce a television commercial to promote men's basketball games.

Another Kennel Club classic was the "No Refs" bag night. After a Thursday night league game where the refs missed some calls that the KC determined had cost the Zags the game, the KC acted quickly in preparation for the next game the following Saturday. They purchased a number of white paper lunch bags and had Art major Tom Bennett ('86) print three vertical black stripes on them to mimic a referee's shirt, and a diagonal red line across the front so as to symbolize "No Refs." They distributed the bags to the KC, and upon the first bad call, they brought out the bags and put them over their heads to show their displeasure.

Chris, being Chris, took it a step further. He actually went out onto the floor during a timeout, with the bag over his head, of course, and confronted the offending referee. Again, only Chris could get away with that. Can you imagine what would happen if a student did that today?

The game environment at the Martin Centre was difficult for all opposing players, but even more so for the poor, unfortunate targets of the Kennel Club. Sometimes that target was selected during warmups, when the KC could see which player(s) reacted to their pregame "engagements," but just as often the selection was made in advance—at the pregame function—when the research done on the opposing roster could be discussed.

All this research was done the old-fashioned way, by reaching out to friends of friends, or friends of players on opposing teams. That is all we had at the time and we made it work.

Some of the research was easy; all that had to be done was to read the local newspaper, like when three Eastern Washington

Left: Former GU Head Coach Jay Hillock was known for exagerrated body language and polyester suits.

Right: When Hillock returned to the Martin Centre as an assistant at LMU, John Webber, Tim O'Neil, and Chris McGahan siezed the opportunity to stage a Hillock look-alike show (pictured here in The Spokesman-Review's *game recap.) Behind the look-alikes are Pete Winning, Pat Mulligan, Jeff Zenier, and John Hyland.*

University basketball players were arrested on petty larceny charges after (allegedly) pilfering 153 cans of soda pop from a Holiday Inn in Pocatello, Idaho, while on a trip to play Idaho State. When the players were introduced prior to their game against Gonzaga just a few weeks later, GU infielder Chris Spring ('87) and the Kennel Club were prepared. As the offending players were being introduced, Spring wheeled a hand truck stacked high with cases of soda to the middle of the Martin Centre floor for the pop bandits.

Some of the research and the Kennel Club responses were more complicated. *The Seattle Times* told the story of when the KC welcomed Oregon State to the Martin Centre:

> In 1986, Ralph Miller-coached Oregon State — one of the few big schools that would play Gonzaga there — came to town with Brian Brundage, a forward who had redeemed his life after being involved in an auto theft as a youth.
>
> That didn't dissuade The Kennel crowd. As [GU coach Dan] Fitzgerald tells it, sometime before warmups, here came 'three guys dressed in prison garb, with a ball and chain, pounding on a fender. God, Ralph was ticked.'

Gonzaga baseball player Dan Beach recalls that, much like Pepperdine's basketball team, the Oregon State basketball players remembered the razzing they took at GU from the Kennel Club, and returned the favor when baseball season rolled around.

"The KC bothered Oregon State's Gary Payton so much" Beach says, "that when baseball season came around, and we were playing our usual Pac-10 North game in Corvallis, Payton and some of his teammates not only showed up to the game to heckle

1985 Men's Baseball Team. Front Row, left to right: Coaches Steve Brown, Steve Hertz, Eric Frey. Second Row: Chris Spring, Jeff Cummins, Dave Rainey, Danny Morris, Ron Davis, Scott Burkhardt, Pete Winning, Clete Wise, Chris McGahan. Third Row: Bruce Molina, Kevin Toliver, Dan Murphy, Mike De-Benedetti, Reed Armijo, John Hyland, Jeff Zenier, Gregg Harris. Back Row: Trainer Steve DeLong, Cass Gebbers, Danny Roe, Steve Suarez, Dan Beach, Vince Barranco, Shane McClary, Tom Bennett, Tim O'Neil, Manager Mike Shields. Not Pictured: Jeff Hainline.

33

us, they laid down on top of our dugout, peeked over the top and were looking at us upside down and telling us that 'this is payback for basketball season!'"

Although sometimes targets were selected in advance due to some piece of intel the KC had uncovered, most of the time the target was simply selected if we thought we could get into his head—one of those "rabbits" who would listen to the crowd and it would affect their play. For those poor souls, the visit to Gonzaga must have been a nightmare. Every time they touched the ball the KC would implore them to "Shoot! Shoot!" to verbalize our belief that they wouldn't make it. If they shot and missed, they would hear it even louder the next time they touched the ball. And if they made it to the free throw line, they were really in for it. The Kennel Club was notorious for chanting "Bounce!" every time the free throw shooter would dribble, and "Miss!" at the exact moment he shot the ball.

AND A MOMENT LATER, Silas Melson, Zach Norvell Jr. and Josh Perkins all went diving for a loose ball directly in front of [Mark] Few, in a pattern recalling the old baseball core of the Kennel Club spelling out "Z-A-G-S" with their flying bodies at timeouts.

John Blanchette
The Spokesman-Review (2017)

The Kennel Club had some fun with coaches as well, especially when former GU head coach Jay Hillock returned as an assistant to head coach Paul Westhead of Loyola Marymount. John Webber, Tim O'Neil and Chris McGahan went to a thrift store to pick up the "Jay Hillock attire" of brown polyester pants and a cream colored dress shirt. Throughout the game, they would drop to their knees, just as Coach Hillock would, and imitate his antics. The next day's edition of *The Spokesman-Review* featured a photo of the three of them at the game.

Coach Hillock had been the head coach at GU when the Kennel Club started; he knew the guys were just having fun with him. In fact, he made a point of coming over to his imitators after the game to shake their hands and have a good laugh with them.

Another part of the baseball team's KC legacy was the human spell-out. Center court spell-outs of "G-O-N-Z-A-G-A" or "Z-A-G-S" (depending on how much time was left during a timeout) were regularly performed by the likes of Tim O'Neil, Jeff Cummins, John Hyland, Jeff Zenier, Pete Winning and Chris McGahan. There was no intricate plan of who would form each part of each letter, and the lack of synchronization made it even better.

Maybe the reason baseball players were so into supporting the basketball team was that they shared the experience as athletes and were friends with the basketball players. In the 1980s Gonzaga sporting events weren't sold out, the teams didn't play on TV every week, and fans didn't greet basketball players at the airport (or the baseball team upon return from a 24-hour bus trip). So if GU athletes wanted to play in a "big-time" environment, they had to generate some of the excitement themselves.

Dan Beach remembers that "a lot of the baseball and basketball players in those days were friends and roommates. So it was actually very natural that we were rooting for them during their season, and they in turn came out to a lot of our games and did the same for us."

Kennel Club solicits membership

The Kennel Club is looking for members. The club is a non-profit organization on the Gonzaga University campus whose function is to support GU's athletic teams, i.e. promote spirit at basketball games. Anyone can become a member. The only requirement is to purchase a club T-shirt. Those interested in the Kennel Club need to contact either Pete Winning or Jeff Zenier.

In November of 1985, the Kennel Club recruited new members by advertising in The Gonzaga Bulletin.

Beach continued, "I remember when Fitz and the basketball team marched up to the Day Court where we were holding winter practice, and the entire group was clapping in unison. Coach Hertz stopped practice so that Fitz could talk to the baseball team. He told us that they had reviewed the basketball game film from a couple nights earlier and figured that the Kennel Club had specifically factored into about six points for the Zags, due to some technical fouls given the other team's players and their coach who had gotten so annoyed at the KC that they'd been T'd up, made a bad pass, etc. That is when Fitz presented us with the first set of Kennel Club shirts that had '6th Man' printed in large letters on the back."

So while the Kennel Club was initially a merger of two distinct groups, the baseball team really took the lead beginning in 1985-86. I truly believe the Kennel Club would have gone the way of the Snake Pit (i.e., lasted only a couple of years) had the baseball team not been involved early on. Not only were the players funny, creative and completely into it, but the team had representatives from every class so that the traditions lived on after the co-founders graduated.

GOING TO THE DOGS

In the fall of 1987, I returned to Gonzaga to pursue a master's degree in Athletics Administration. One of the first things I did was to reconnect with Dale Goodwin, who had been the Sports Information Director and unofficial wrangler of the Kennel Club. In the early years of the KC, on the rare occasion (depending on your perspective) · we got out of hand, he had taken on the unenviable task of trying to put us back into our cage. Dale had the respect of everyone in our group, so when he came to us during a game—many times with a smile on his face—we would try to dial it back a notch or two.

Perhaps seeing an opportunity to relieve himself of that thankless duty, Dale asked if I would be the "graduate advisor" to the Kennel Club. I accepted the offer without considering the ramifications. Instead of being one of the instigators, one of those joining in on the chants and taunts, and the one calling out the letters of a spell-out, I would be the one who the coaches and administrators looked to (literally) when the KC did something outside the acceptable norm, which was at least once per game.

Dale also arranged for the two of us to meet with one of his corporate contacts at Blue Mountain Pet Foods. After having only baseball hitting shirts for the 1985-86 season and then Fitz helping with the 1986-87 shirts, Dale sold Blue Mountain on becoming the Kennel Club's first-ever corporate sponsor. In exchange for placing their brand on the back of the KC shirts, along with the tagline "Going to the Dogs," Blue Mountain gave the KC $1,000 to underwrite the cost of the shirts for the 1987-88 season, and the 6th Man moniker moved to the sleeve.

The Kennel Club, for their part of the bargain, agreed to conduct a pet food drive in support of a Spokane animal shelter. Dale created a press release promoting Blue Mountain's sponsorship of the home game against the University of San Diego, with fans receiving half-off the ticket price in exchange for a donated can or bag of pet food. About 400 pounds of pet food was collected, and the event was even mentioned in the "Short Shots" section of the February 1, 1988, issue of *Sports Illustrated*.

I know this must seem like small potatoes to the Kennel Clubbers of today, but Gonzaga was in the midst of a 14-14 season (5-9 in the WCC) in 1988, and the Zags were nowhere near *SI*'s Top 20 team rankings. The fact that just a Kennel Club mention in the "Short Shots" section of *Sports Illustrated* was a big deal, while the Zags not being anywhere near the Top 20 was not, ought to tell you how far the Kennel Club and Gonzaga basketball have come in the last 30 years.

Blue Mountain wasn't the last sponsor of the Kennel Club shirt, which continued to gain praise and scrutiny alike. Pet food giant Alpo acquired Blue Mountain, and different Alpo brands were featured on the back of the Kennel Club shirts over the next few years. During this time, Alpo also served as title sponsor to a Gonzaga-based basketball tournament, The Alpo Inland Northwest Classic.

Bayou Brewing opted in as KC shirt sponsor for a year or two, as did Kimmel Athletics (who produced the shirts), Arny's, Papa John's Pizza and George Gee Automotive in the Spokane Valley were all pleased to see their name across the backs or sleeves of the Kennel Club shirts, worn at every home game.

One of the first things we did after formalizing the group and securing its first corporate sponsor was to integrate the Kennel Club; up until that point its "membership" had been exclusively male. The all-male nature of the group wasn't a conscious decision anyone had made. Rather, it was a result of the "club" being founded by a group of male roommates, our closest male friends, and the baseball team. Women had been a part of the rowdiness from the start—dating back to the "painted faces crew" in 1984— they only lacked the formalities of owning a KC shirt and being an active part of the on-court proceedings. But those were two pretty big shortcomings. The administration made it clear that

With his typical cleverness, The Spokesman-Review reporter John Blanchette christened KC co-founders and baseball players Tim O'Neil and Jeff Zenier "Dr. Heckle and Mr. Chide." This article from January 31, 1987, was one of the first full-length features on the Kennel Club.

Staff photo by STEVE THOMPSON

Gonzaga's raucous Kennel Club leaves some opposing coaches and players barking about having to play in Spokane.

Kennel Club takes a rare breed

By John Blanchette
Staff writer

Consider this an entrance exam.

The old college team is down by seven midway through the first half. Shots won't fall, fouls come easy. The visiting team is hitting everything it puts up, and the coach — a tough, savvy, banty rooster type with a fiery glare, a hard-set jaw and a mid-section betraying middle age — is up working the refs, generally to his advantage.

You consider yourself among the most loyal of fans. From the bleachers, you:

A) Start a cheer of "Two bits, four bits, six bits, a dollar ..."

B) Keep quiet and hope things get better.

C) Begin chanting at the opposing coach, "Mix in a salad! Mix in a salad!"

If you said A, you'll be asked to repeat grades 9 through 12. If you said B, you are probably majoring in peer group and certainly will vote Republican in the next election.

If you said C, the Kennel Club wants you.

Duke, it's not. The Pit, it's not. Even Montana, it's not.

But Gonzaga University's Martin Centre — or Kennedy Pavilion as it was known until this winter — is, by general if not unanimous acclaim, the toughest place to play in the West Coast Athletic Conference.

That may not be saying much. WCAC basketball is not the worst-attended college game in the land, but the ACC is safe. Average crowds last year were 2,116, or 23rd out of 32 NCAA Division I conferences. One arena, the University of San Diego's Sports Center, is fronted by iron gates and a sparkling swimming pool and has the look of a Spanish castle. On the outside. Inside, it's a dreary little gym with 2,500 seats that makes you want to be outside — which, in its own way, makes it a tough place to play.

On the other end of the scale, Portland's new Chiles Center, completed two years ago, is a state-of-the-art 5,000-seat dome, but the Pilots' success in the last few years has been indifferent at best and, as they say, plenty of good seats are still available.

Gonzaga doesn't sell out its recently renovated barn often, either. The members of the Kennel Club do not have to camp out at ticket manager Wilma Brickner's desk just to get the choice seats.

But that doesn't mean they wouldn't. There are a lot of factors in making Martin Centre a tough place for a visiting team to win a game. Start with the home team. This year, the Bulldogs' record happens to be 14-5, but even if it's 5-14, their style is relentlessly physical, dogged and designed to keep you at anything but your best.

Then there's the trip. Six of the WCAC's tourists stay year-round at the Hotel California, and the last thing they want to do in January and February is fly to Spokane for the winter carnival. As Bulldog coach Dan Fitzgerald says, "On game day, I wake up hoping it's 10 degrees with a foot of snow on the ground."

And then there's the Kennel Club.

It's not a big organization, at least yet, and not the first of its kind. By and large, the guys sporting Kennel Club T-Shirts on game night in the winter are in Bulldog baseball uniforms in the spring. But membership is very much open, as long as you live up — or down, if you prefer — to certain standards. You don't have to play baseball, even.

It's just that these young men have taken the bull — the Bulldogs? — by the horns, so to speak.

They aren't coaches, really, or captains, or even elected officers. But Kennel Clubbers Tim O'Neil and Jeff Zenier should have titles, so here goes:

(See Club on page 3)

Thanks to the excellent supprt of Dale Goodwin, 1987-88 saw the introduction of the first shirt with a corporate sponsor. We also added the "6th Man" tagline on the sleeve.

After formalizing the KC's organizational status on campus for the 1987-88 season, we quickly realized that women were just as passionate about Zag basketball as we were. Since then, seven women have served as KC Presidents:

Jodi Elmose, Co-President (2002-03)
Kathryn McGoffin, President (2011-12)
Trang Nguyen, President (2013-14)
Sara Wendland, President (2014-15)
Sharon Greer, President (2015-16)
Claire Murphy, President (2017-18)
Taylor Woods, President (2018-19)

Right: Left to right: Siobhan McDonald ('01), Anna Davidson ('01), Emilee Steckler ('01), and Jenny Scott ('01) attend a game during the 1999-2000 season.

Club——

(Continued from page 1)

O'Neil is Dr. Heckle. Zenier is Mr. Chide.

"We had a fine recruiting year," Zenier reports. "We've got a lot of good young freshmen with a lot of potential, which is important because we've lost a few veterans to maturity."

In athletics, the legs go first. In heckling, it's immaturity.

"A couple good transfers came in, too," adds O'Neil. "What's good is that you don't have to sit out a year. The NCAA rules are kind of loose as far as that goes."

Both four-year Kennelmen, O'Neil and Zenier claim to be high school All-Americans who chose Gonzaga because of its athletic facilities.

"It was a tough decision to go here or to UCLA," insists O'Neil. "But there's definitely more potential here than at Pauley."

Echoes Zenier, "I took a lot of recruiting trips, but when I saw I'd be able to be right on the floor here, well, that was it. The facility definitely had a lot to do with it. I'd hate to find myself seven rows up behind the press table. They're not going to hear you from up there, anyway."

What about targets? Any criteria?

"We like to pick out a guy early," explains Zenier. "He might have six knee braces, he might have his socks pulled up to his knees, he might look like he just came out of Mad magazine."

"Maybe it's just a name," says O'Neil. "Sometimes we'll dip into the press guide a little bit. We like personal information."

Coaches?

"Relatively speaking," O'Neil claims, "we don't get on them much. But if they have an interest in us, we have an obligation to be good hosts. We like Jack Avina of Portland. And we have a lot of respect for Paul Westhead because he's been in the NBA."

"But that might drop a little bit in a couple of weeks," Zenier assures us.

When former Gonzaga head coach Jay Hillock returned as a Loyola Marymount assistant last year, the club was ready with the Jay Hillock Look-Alike Night — with O'Neil, Chris McGahan and John Weber doing the impersonations.

Do they have an All-Rag Team?

"Nick Vanos, the old Santa Clara center would have to be on it," says Zenier. "We called him Herman Munster. He said in the paper this was the toughest place to play."

"Jose Ortiz of Oregon State," O'Neil offers. "(OSU's Brian) Brundage handled it well, but Ortiz got all bent out of shape."

"Jerome Hall of Eastern," says Zenier. "We got him on a road game. And Keith Smith of Loyola. He was the biggest rabbit of all time."

"There is absolutely nothing wrong with noisy things. All our parents were wrong."
— Charlie Pierce

Staff photo by DAN PELLE

'The crowd is so incredible,' says GU's Jim McPhee. 'It gets you so fired up . . . '

Predictably, the Kennel Club's increased vocal presence at this year's games has triggered the usual cluck-clucking about "appropriate behavior," both on campus and in the opposite bleachers.

And true, occasionally the limits of good taste are stretched.

But it's fairly traditional, if you get right down to it. The hi-jinx at Duke (where North Carolina's Mike O'Koren was once taunted with a banner proclaiming him "Oxy-1000 Poster Child") and at Tennessee (where Auburn's Charles Barkley was delivered a pizza in the layup line), among other places, often cuts close to cruel. Compared to hurling 1,000 pair of ladies' underwear at an alleged sex offender, which also happened at Duke, "Mix in a salad!" is hitting above the belt.

The club did have a member dressed as a prison inmate to greet OSU's Brundage, who was once convicted of robbery. Liberals winced, but it got the Kennel Club a mention in People magazine.

The Kennel could probably cool the racial inferences, but it must be said that they heckle without regard to race, creed or color. Everyone gets in.

They aren't much into signs or posters, nor have they come up with the killer joke yet. They do have a nice bodies-flying, spell-out routine ("but we're always losing a guy every week," complains

O'Neil). In all honesty, they probably aren't ready to play the big room, but what they lack in sophistication, they make up for in enthusiasm.

And the people whose votes should count the most — GU's players — are unanimous.

"The crowd is so incredible," says leading scorer Jim McPhee, who is hardly a potential Hell's Angel. "It gets you so fired up that you just want to come out and bury a team. Sometimes, your adrenaline is too high."

"They are really wild," says guard Paul Walker. "Really wild."

Outside of some artificially fueled hockey fans, that's a rarity in this part of the country — even in other parts of GU's gym. If nothing else, the Kennel would like their enthusiasm, if not their material, to rub off.

Fitzgerald, too, approves — though he might blanch at an occasional bark from the Kennel. He even popped for the T-shirts.

"The only thing I told them is to raise hell with class," Fitzgerald says, "and don't disrupt the game. They can't be doing that. Enthusiasm is rarely perfect, and I think you need a little of that here. This isn't the Silicon Valley. Our guys aren't the sweaters-tied-around-the-neck type.

"Besides, if all you get out of college is a degree, you've been cheated."

they wanted the club to represent a true cross-section of the University, and that we were going to have to extend the support the KC had provided to sports beyond men's basketball as well.

We held our first open meeting of the "new" Kennel Club in what was then the Bulldog Club room in the Martin Centre. The room was packed. Not only was the entire baseball team there, but most of the volleyball team and other student-athletes were as well.

As the advisor, one of the things I suggested the club do was to elect officers. If my memory serves me, both nominations and a vote took place that night. Bob Finn, who grew up in Spokane and played baseball at West Valley High School and Eastern Washington University before transferring to Gonzaga, was elected the first President of the Kennel Club. Together, we laid out the expectations of the group; they included attendance at all men's basketball games, and attendance at 50% of women's basketball, volleyball and baseball home games. Each person who filled out a membership card committing to that attendance received a free KC shirt.

Part of me was excited about the growth of the KC, but a bigger part of me felt that by formalizing the group we would lose the spontaneity and the creativity that had made it special. I know others in the room that night felt the same way—particularly a few members of the baseball team—and I think some of them held me responsible for "selling out" to the administration, and maybe I did.

As that season began, I remember making the conscious decision to sit on the upper level of the season ticket holder (south) side of the Martin Centre—opposite the student section—to distance myself from the group. After being involved in every aspect of the Kennel Club for its first two years, it was a hard thing to do. By the end of that season, I quit coming to games altogether because to tell the same people I had been standing beside for two years that they could no longer do what I had done felt very hypocritical.

So, as I took a step back from the Kennel Club, Tim O'Neil and Jeff Zenier were two of the GU baseball players who stepped into untitled leadership roles. Those two guys became so notorious that *The Spokesman-Review* reporter John Blanchette even gave O'Neil and Zenier "titles" in an article that appeared in the January 31, 1987 edition of the newspaper's sports section: Dr. Heckle and Mr. Chide.

Left to right: Early Kennel Clubbers Joe Roberts, Mike Shields, Tony Rose (partially obscured) and Bob Twiss (plaid shirt) lead the Kennedy Pavilion crowd in a chant. Top left, the Kennedy Pavilion had a viewing balcony before a remodel in the late 1980s.

I was at a game [recently], and as I watched that pulsating section, wreaking all sorts of havoc, I thought, "Nobody really knows, but I'm actually a MEMBER of that club, even though I'm a Wazzu Coug! And you know what? I'm proud to be a member."

Eric Johnson
Former KREM-TV sportscaster

THANK YOU, SIR, MAY I HAVE ANOTHER?!

John Blanchette wasn't the only journalist to take notice. Eric Johnson was a sportscaster at KREM-TV in Spokane in the late '80s when he contacted the Athletics department about doing a behind-the-scenes story on the Kennel Club. He was put in touch with co-founders Tim O'Neil and Chris McGahan.

As part of the story, Johnson told O'Neil and McGahan he wanted to become a full member of the group. Although there were no initiation rites to become a member, the two of course told Johnson there were. He arrived at a KC party about two hours before game time, consumed a couple of adult beverages in shotgun fashion, and then was put through various rituals he was told were required of every member. Among them, he "had" to crawl on his hands and knees through a "hack line" where dozens of Kennel Clubbers lined up to take their "hacks" at the future Emmy winner. I was amazed at how good a sport he was being about it, because he got abused!

Eventually, O'Neil and McGahan felt he had jumped through enough hoops to qualify for membership and presented him with his very own KC shirt. Johnson's report, along with some interviews, footage from the KC party and his participation with the KC during the game, appeared in Johnson's sports segment of KREM's newscast the following night.

To my knowledge, Eric is the only media figure who is also an honorary Kennel Clubber. I'm sure he is as proud of that as he is of his more than 40 Regional Emmy Awards and the three National Edward R. Murrow Awards he had received as of 2017. He is currently the weeknight news anchor for ABC affiliate KOMO-TV in Seattle.

Kennel Club gives Support to 'Dogs

Marc Ruckwardt
Staff Writer

The mere mention of the Gonzaga Athletic Centre strikes fear into the hearts of opposing teams. It is known to many as the loudest, rowdiest and toughest place to play in the Western Coast Athletic Conference.

One of the major reasons for this is due to the efforts of the infamous Kennel Club. The Kennel Club was started last season by Mike Shields, who is known by the faithfuls as the "Founding Father."

There are, however, many differences this year from last. One of the main changes is it used to be of elite membership and this year it is open to anyone who is interested.

Still another is the absence of Chris McGahan, who was last year's ringleader.

"Chris could get the crowd going and it isn't as rad this year as he graduated and is a tough act to follow," said Tim O'Neil, a current member of the club.

However, McGahan did return this year for the Loyola Marymount game to give the fans a taste of last season and also to razz Jay Hillock, Gonzaga's head coach a year ago and an assistant on Loyola's staff.

What do the Kennel Club members do?

"We see how many beers we can drink before the game and have a good time," O'Neil said. "A lot of our good friends are on the basketball team and we just want to give them a little incentive to play harder, knowing that we're behind them."

O'Neil ended by saying that although the Bulldogs started out with three straight losses, the Kennel Club members never gave up on the team.

"They won't give up so we don't either."

The team has since won three consecutive games.

Just two years after its launch, the Kennel Club had become a campus phenomenon. The Gonzaga Bulletin featured the KC in this article from February 6, 1986.

The Kennel Club was the same awesome animal as it is today, just on a different scale. And I think the smaller scale from the Kennedy Pavilion/Martin Centre era allowed for more organized creativity, particularly against the specific players or coaches they targeted.

Jim McPhee
Four-time All-Conference selection (1986-90)

THE KENNEL CLUB SITS DOWN

In 1988, Loyola Marymount came to town with Hank Gathers and Bo Kimble leading the way. This was the first season the pair played for the Lions after transferring from USC, and Paul Westhead's third season as head coach at LMU after NBA stops with the Chicago Bulls and the Los Angeles Lakers, where he'd won an NBA title with Magic Johnson and Kareem Abdul-Jabbar.

At that time, the GU Athletics department offices were on the third floor of the Martin Centre. Some of those offices had windows overlooking the basketball court. I remember standing in the office of John Preston, GU's then-Director of Athletic Development, and watching LMU practice on the day prior to the game. Toward the end of practice, the Lions broke off into pairs for a 3-point shooting drill, one rebounding for the other. Gathers and Kimble were paired up at a basket just below my third floor perch. I watched in awe as they moved at game speed and let it fly from behind the 19-foot 9-inch arc. I vividly recall counting off their shots: They didn't miss a single one; the duo drilled 32 in a row!

Westhead's beyond up-tempo, run-and-gun style of play was a perfect fit for Gathers and Kimble, who were blue-chip recruits coming out of Dobbins Tech in North Philadelphia, but they were only at LMU because they had lasted just one year at USC under coach George Raveling.

Although he led the nation in scoring in 1988-89 with over 32 points per game, Gathers shot just 56% from the free throw line. Compounding his poor results at the line was the Kennel Club chant of "George was right! George was right!" which was in reference to Raveling having released Gathers and Kimble from their scholarships at USC.

The Kennel Club was also on LMU guard and two-sport star Enoch Simmons pretty good, chanting "E-wok! E-wok!" at him (due to the similarity between Simmons' first name and the furry creatures from *Star Wars*) during pregame warmups, and having an on-going "conversation" with him during the game itself.

Fairly early in the game, as Simmons was bringing the ball up the court, he purposefully dribbled over by the Kennel Club, who were all standing along the sideline, and clearly said, "Watch this..." He then proceeded to give the GU defender what I can only describe as a "Shake & Bake" move, drove past him down the lane to the basket and delivered a powerful tomahawk dunk. As he trotted back down the court, he shot the KC a look that I interpreted as him saying, "I can do that any time I want" and, in unison, the entire Kennel Club sat down. That's the only time I've ever seen or heard about the KC sitting down during a game.

A couple of years later, I was the assistant general manager of the Modesto A's—the Oakland A's California League affiliate. I was checking out equipment to the players on their first day in town, and in walked Enoch Simmons, who had been playing in the A's minor league system for a few years at that point. I asked if he remembered that Gonzaga game, and he said, "Yeah, I shut you guys up pretty good."

Yes, he did.

In 1988-89, Hank Gathers became the second player in the history of NCAA Division I basketball to lead the nation in both scoring and rebounding in a single season (Wichita State's Xavier McDaniel was the first to achieve that feat in 1984-85). Tragically, Gathers died during a WCC Tournament semifinal game versus the University of Portland on March 4, 1990 (LMU had beaten Gonzaga 121-84 in a tournament quarterfinal game the day before). The cause of death was hypertrophic cardiomyopathy.

After famously honoring his fallen teammate by shooting his free-throws with his left hand (just as Hank had done) during the Lions emotional, Elite Eight run through the 1990 NCAA Tournament, Bo Kimble was selected with the 8th pick of the 1990 NBA Draft by the Los Angeles Clippers.

I don't remember any less enthusiasm, but there probably was a natural drop-off given that there was objectively less to cheer about than in other years. Hanging in there the way they did must have been difficult for the Kennel Club. Very difficult. Eight-and-twenty difficult.

Jim McPhee
#2 on Gonzaga's career scoring list

GROUND 'ZERO'

In my opinion, the biggest threat to the Kennel Club's survival beyond its infancy was the nightmare season of 1989-90. The Zags had just come off of a 14-14 season the year before, and were about to embark on a schedule that would result in their worst record (8-20 overall; 3-11 in the WCC) in nearly 40 years.

I challenge anyone who thinks that the Kennel Club is simply a by-product of Gonzaga basketball's rise to national prominence to take a look at the GU record book. In the six seasons that encompass the Kennel Club's creation and formalization (1984-90), the Zags' combined record was 86-82 (.512), and the season before the KC officially came into being (1983-84), their record was 17-11. During that same timespan, their average finish was fifth place, or the bottom half of the then-eight-team conference.

So how does a group of students maintain their enthusiasm during a six-year period when the team is losing as often as it is winning? I think it speaks not only to the resiliency of young people, but also to the spirit of the Kennel Club. For better or worse, we love the Zags!

Jim Fitzgerald, KC President and a captain on the GU baseball team at the time, put it this way:

> Back then, GU basketball was 'it' for us. Gonzaga didn't have a football program, so basketball games were the thing to do on Thursday and Saturday nights. The Kennel Club was there regardless of the team record. Today, I don't think any old Kennel Club members would remember what our

record was back then. It didn't matter. It was never 'the GU basketball team lost last night, it was WE lost last night.' We went to the games because those players were in class with us, we saw them walking around campus and we had dinner together in the COG (the dining hall and campus center). GU was one big family. The greatest thing about GU back then was that you knew everybody; the worst thing about GU back then was that you knew everybody. Basketball players couldn't hide on campus, but they could count on the Kennel Club being front and center before tipoff of every game.

One of the few bright spots in that season was the play of senior Jim McPhee. Despite being the second leading scorer in the history of the GU program, behind the legendary Frank Burgess, whose retired #44 hangs in the rafters at McCarthey Athletic Center, I believe Jim is one of the most overlooked and underrated players in the history of Gonzaga basketball. I think that is largely because he played on middle-of-the-pack teams in the era after John Stockton, before Gonzaga's NIT and NCAA teams of the mid-90s, and during that brief period in the late '80s when Loyola Marymount overshadowed every program on the west coast except UNLV.

Another reason Jim McPhee seemed to fly under the radar may have been because he was a lot like John Stockton; neither was real flashy in his play or demeanor; they both were the type of guy who just got the job done (well) and went home. In other words, they were the quintessential Zags in the Dan Fitzgerald era.

Having said all that, if I were a coach and needed someone to knock down a mid-range jumper in a clutch situation, Jim McPhee would be my choice over any other GU player, past or present.

McPhee could flat-out shoot. To my admittedly amateur eye, his form was flawless. He averaged a career-high 23.6 points per game in 1989-90. In one eight-day stretch, he scored 42 points in each of two games versus nationally-ranked Loyola Marymount. As further evidence of how difficult that season was for GU, consider that the McPhee-led Zags scored 100 points in the first of those two games against the Lions, and still lost by 44 points!

While the pace of play in games with LMU was exhausting, there were players who chose to use some of their energy to have a "dialogue" with Kennel Club. "I remember players that would swear at the Kennel Club after they scored," McPhee said. "I liked that they were spending energy on something besides trying to

Among the KC's many exploits in the late '80s was a Fitz look-alike night.

Standing, left to right, Tim Shields, Mark Lally, Bill Bartell, Mark Schumock, Brian Gabert, Greg Hanss. Kneeling Tom Pivonka.

Before his passing in 2002, Reverend Anthony Lehmann, SJ, better known simply as "Father Tony," was a fixture at the end of the bench for the Gonzaga men's basketball team. He bettered the life of every person he came in touch with at GU and around the world. In his memory sits a bronze of his empty chair at McCarthey Athletic Center. Engraved on the chair are the words Father Tony used at the end every conversation:

"To be continued..."

When he wasn't with the team, or supporting students around campus, Father Tony might occassionally be seen "blessing the keg" at one social function or another.

Gonzaga Career Points Leaders

	Name	Points	Years
1.	Frank Burgess	2,196	1959-61
2.	Jim McPhee	2,015	1986-90
3.	Adam Morrison	1,867	2004-06
4.	Elias Harris	1,857	2009-13
5.	Kevin Pangos	1,824	2012-15
6.	Matt Santangelo	1,810	1997-00
7.	Ronny Turiaf	1,723	2002-05
8.	Matt Bouldin	1,683	2007-10
9.	Blake Stepp	1,670	2001-04
10.	Jeff Brown	1,646	1992-94

Frank Burgess (top) and Jim McPhee still top the Zags all-time career scoring list.

beat us. Only Hank Gathers seemed to really enjoy jawing with the Kennel Club. They would get after each other—full-on trash talking conversations during the game. But there was a lot of mutual respect between the Kennel Club and Hank. They both looked forward to it."

Alongside the jawing, the Kennel Club maintained the creativity of the founding group. McPhee remembers some theme nights: "One night they dressed up as Fitz. One night they dressed up as Father Tony [Lehmann]. Once they dressed up as the opposing coach and mimicked his every move—and that coach got T'd up that night. One minute the Kennel Club would unleash a wall of sound on everyone, and then the next minute they'd isolate a single player and poke at his innermost insecurity. The research they did on other teams' players was impressive, especially pre-internet/social media."

So while the team struggled, the Kennel Club legend continued to grow. Jim Fitzgerald cites this exchange with an official that season: "During one game, the Kennel Club was all over a referee about missed calls and calling too many fouls against GU. After the game was over, that ref walked over to the student section and handed me a piece of paper with an address on it. He said, 'I live in California and my son would love one of those Kennel Club shirts, could you mail one to me?' I was stunned that after we rode him the entire game, he would want to talk to us. I told him I would see if we had any extra T-shirts. I did find one and mailed it to him with a short note stating that I hoped his son enjoyed the shirt and, yes, I was the nephew of Dan Fitzgerald."

"From then on, when he returned to GU to work a game, he would give me a quick eye wink," Jim Fitzgerald said. "I want to believe he didn't make a call against GU in our gym from that point forward, but I don't know if that would be factual."

The 1989-90 season marked a turning point for GU basketball. The talented group of freshmen who redshirted that year would go on to become the core of a team that finished the 1993-94 season with a 22-8 record, captured GU's first WCC title, and won Gonzaga's first-ever postseason tournament game, an 80-76 win at Stanford in the first round of the 1994 National Invitation Tournament (NIT). That NIT win served as the jumping off point for the program. The next season (1994-95) the Zags played in their first-ever NCAA tournament, and the program and the Kennel Club have experienced exponential growth ever since.

That group of redshirt freshmen and transfers could have made a huge difference in the outcome of Jim McPhee's final season with the Zags. Being the humble person he is, though, McPhee said, "When people say that I played any part in the future success of the program I agree only insofar as my final year's team was the 'zero' in that 180 degree turn of Gonzaga hoops."

GU MEN'S BASKETBALL RECORD (1984-90)

Season	W-L Record	WCAC Finish
1984-85	15-13	5th
1985-86	15-13	4th
1986-87	18-10	2nd
1987-88	16-12	5th
1988-89	14-14	6th
1989-90	8-20	8th
1984-90	86-82 (.512)	

Though difficult for newer fans to imagine, the Kennel Club was born and grew during a time when the team was merely middle of the pack in the then-WCAC.

49

"Du bist nicht gut"
(Translation: "You are not good.")

Kennel Club sign at a 1993 exhibition versus TTL Bamberg, a German professional team. Now Brose Bamberg, their 2018 roster included former Zag and German native Elias Harris.

THE BREAK-THROUGH YEARS

Rebounding from the 8-20 season in 1989-90, the Zags averaged more than 17 wins a year, including their first 20-win season in a quarter-century, over the following three seasons. By the time the 1993-94 season rolled around, the seniors who were redshirt freshman during the disastrous season of 1989-90—players like Geoff Goss, Matt Stanford and Scott Spink, along with junior John Rillie and UW transfer Jeff Brown (all of whom were recruited to play for the Zags by GU's trio of young assistants Dan Monson, Mark Few and Bill Grier)—were ready to make their mark on the program.

The KC President in 1993-94 was Brian Girardot. His sister Marie ('84) and his brother Steve ('88) had also attended GU. Like many "Gonzaga families," including my own, with multiple siblings or generations attending the University, Brian chose to come to GU because of the experiences his older sister and brother had while in Spokane. Girardot says that in the mid-90s Gonzaga was still "small enough that there were no cliques; everyone was friends. The closest thing I can compare to the camaraderie I experienced in the military was my time in the Kennel Club."

The closeness between the student-athletes and the rest of the student body is best evidenced by the fact that KC leaders often lived with or were close friends with GU basketball players or other athletes. "We weren't pulling for our team as much as we were pulling for our pals," Girardot said.

Jeff Brown recalls it this way:

> One of the many great parts of Gonzaga is the lack of any formal Greek system—freshman and sophomore students are all living in dorms and there is a tremendous sense of community and inclusion. The fact that many of your good friends were members of the Kennel Club created a true sense of campus camaraderie. Nothing was better than seeing your friends and classmates bonding together to make The Kennel the incredibly tough place to play as it was and continues to be. It is difficult to describe the feeling and emotions of running through the KC before or after a game with the very vocal support of the campus!

I JUST WANT TWO THINGS from the Pilots: First, an upper-half WCC team. Second, an end to those damn "THIS IS OUR HOUSE" chants from the Kennel Club at the Chiles Center every friggin' year!

PilotNation.net
University of Portland men's basketball message board (2008)

While the 1993-94 Zags stumbled out of the gate, the Kennel Club started in mid-season form when San Jose State came to the Martin Centre amidst rumors of some financial improprieties. The KC painted dollar signs on basketballs and chanted "Write us a check!" during the Spartans' season-opening win over the Zags.

But the Kennel Club wasn't only a factor in Spokane; the group traveled well, too. About 200 KC members road-tripped to Portland for the Zags' annual Rose City battle with the Pilots. Although UP was up by nearly 30 points in the first half, the Zags charged back for a 75-71 win. By the time the game was over, the Kennel Club had taken over the Chiles Center with chants of "Go! Gonzaga! G-O-N-Z-A-G-A!" and "This is our house!" Following their hostile take-over of the Pilots' home court, the KC took over UP's version of Jack & Dan's Tavern—The Twilight Room, or The T-Room as locals call it—and celebrated the win until closing time.

Gonzaga and Pepperdine became true rivals during the 1990s. After losing 12 straight games to the Waves dating back to 1988, the Zags finally broke through with a 63-52 win in the final head-to-head match-up of the 1993 WCC regular season. The next season the Zags swept the Waves for the first time and took home their first-ever WCC title with a 12-2 record.

Girardot, like many KC Presidents, worked at Jack & Dan's and recalls that one of the coaches laid down some cash and told him to keep the drinks coming as long as the money lasted. "Little Gonzaga owned the universe that night," said Girardot.

IT WAS ALWAYS FANTASTIC to have the KC at the WCC Tournament. I have vivid memories of them at Santa Clara my senior year. I was blown away by the number of students who had literally driven all night to make it to the Bay!

Jeff Brown
WCC Player of the Year (1994)

The Kennel Club led a caravan of up to 100 cars heading down to the Bay Area for the WCC Tournament in 1994. Girardot said that every available square inch in his parents' San Jose home was taken up with Kennel Clubbers' sleeping bags. He said the same was true of other Bay Area homes hosting GU students for the tournament, held that year at Santa Clara.

The Zags lost to San Diego in the WCC Tournament semifinals, but their 21-7 record qualified them for their first-ever appearance in the National Invitation Tournament (NIT). GU beat Stanford on their home floor for their first-ever postseason victory, and then traveled to Manhattan, Kansas, for their second-round game against a very good Kansas State team that featured senior Askia Jones, who averaged over 22 points per game.

The Kennel Club hosted "listening parties" at Jack & Dan's for both NIT games. Girardot was working double-duty as KC President and as a Jack & Dan's bartender the night of the Kansas State game. Following the Zags' heart-breaking two-point loss to the Wildcats, Girardot said, "We felt bad for not only our team and our school, we felt bad for our buddies."

In Kansas State's 115–77 victory over Fresno State in the NIT quarterfinals, Askia Jones set the NCAA postseason record of 14 three-point field goals made. His final total of 62 points, including nine consecutive three-point shots spanning the first and second halves, was the second-highest single game scoring output in major college postseason history. Kansas State would lose to Vanderbilt in the NIT semifinals, and Jones would go on to have a professional career spanning nearly two decades, including a brief stint with the NBA's Minnesota Timberwolves.

The 1993-94 season marked a series of firsts: the Zags' first season sweep of Pepperdine, their first WCC title, their first postseason appearance and first postseason win. That team broke down the door, and the GU program has never been the same.

Coming off that high point in program history, the Zags lost four of their top five scorers, including WCC Player of the Year Jeff Brown and first-team all-conference point guard Geoff Goss. Senior-to-be John Rillie, an Australian sharp-shooter who had come to Gonzaga via Tacoma Community College, would be the centerpiece of the Zags' 1994-95 team. Rillie had averaged more than 12 points per game on an astonishing 45% shooting from three-point range during his junior year.

> **WE PLAYED AN EXHIBITION game against an Aussie team (Canberra Cannons). A little-used bench player enters during garbage time with his Canberra jersey on backwards and the Kennel Club starts chanting, "Big number goes on back!"**
>
> John Rillie
> *WCC Tournament MVP (1995)*

At the beginning of the 1994-95 school year, Damon DeRosa ('95) took the reins as KC President. The connection between the team and the Kennel Club was particularly strong during this time because one of DeRosa's housemates, Scott Spink's younger brother Tomson, was a KC member and would later become the club's President during the 1995-96 season. Tomson Spink ('96) had tried out for the team and had been cut. He admits to harboring some anger about not being on the team (his youngest brother Mark would later be a prominent player on the Zags' 1999 Elite Eight team), but he says that he "loved the game and loved the Zags," so leading the KC was a natural outlet for those emotions.

Yet another connection to the team was that DeRosa and his housemates, Spink and Tim Andress ('96), lived with GU player Jason Rubright in what became known as "The Kennel Club House" at 1010 DeSmet. Like many in the Logan neighborhood, the house was built in the early 1900s and had suffered much abuse at the hands of its student tenants over the years. The house's "heating system" was originally a coal-fired furnace with large heating grates in the floor to circulate air upward through the house. Spink recalls being pranked at a party when someone precariously propped the heating grate so that the next person to step on it would fall through it and into the basement. The result was an injury that nearly kept him from that evening's game. But there were good things that happened for Spink at KC parties, too. Tomson met Cara Clark ('96), his future wife, at a pregame function at 1010 DeSmet.

DeRosa recalls that Father Tony Lehmann, SJ—the beloved Gonzaga team chaplain and former Carthusian monk—would regularly come to Kennel Club pre-functions held at their house to interact with students and, of course, to bless the kegs.

Though the team started out a very disappointing 0-6 in WCC play, the "blessed" Kennel Club continued to hold court and made the Martin Centre the toughest place to play in the conference. Only two of those six losses were at home, and they were the only back-to-back home losses in Rillie's three seasons at Gonzaga. The first of the two was to Santa Clara, which broke the Zags' 34-game home winning streak. Only Indiana and UMass had longer home winning streaks at that time. That Santa Clara game was also a preview of things to come for Bronco great, Steve Nash. The future two-time NBA Most Valuable Player scored 35 of his career-high 40 points in the second half to rally SCU to a 73-68 overtime win.

The Kennel Club's impact was very evident to Rillie. In fact, he recalls overhearing an argument between Portland players over who was going to inbound the ball in front of the KC section in a pivotal late-season game at the Martin Centre. Rillie said that one of the Pilots "just flat refused to be the guy to inbound the ball," not wanting to have to deal with a pack of screaming students. Jeff Brown remembers the same being true the year before as he "used to pity the opposing player who had to take the ball out on the sideline directly in front of the KC."

Meanwhile, the Zags rallied from their six-game losing streak to earn the #4 seed in the conference tournament. In wins over San Diego, St. Mary's and Portland, Rillie scored 96 points while making 20 of 28 three-pointers—a torrid 71.4%.

Dan Fitzgerald's instructions to his team at the 1995 WCC Tournament while shave-headed, gunner-from-down-under, Rillie was on his 3-point shooting streak were classic Fitz, "Get the round thing to the bald thing." Rillie's performance earned him MVP honors and sent Gonzaga to its first NCAA Tournament.

The little-known Zags entered the 1995 NCAA Tournament with a WCC title and a 22-8 record. For that, they were awarded a #14 seed and matched up with the #3 seed in the West Region, Maryland. The Terrapins were led by Joe Smith, a consensus All-American and Naismith College Player of the Year, who would later become the #1 overall selection in the 1995 NBA Draft by the Golden State Warriors. Asked about the matchup with Maryland and its All-American center, Fitzgerald quipped, "It's not David and Goliath, but it might be the prelim."

Jason Rubright, housemate of then-KC President Damon DeRosa and future KC President Tomson Spink, would have the responsibility of guarding Smith. Rubright and the Zags held Smith to just nine points (11 points under his season average), but Maryland beat the Zags, 87-63 to end GU's first ever NCAA Tournament appearance.

Tomson, who earned a degree in Civil Engineering from Gonzaga, would eventually come full circle and return to GU as an employee. He was a project manager for Spokane's Garco Construction in the design and build-out of McCarthey Athletic Center (MAC), and was then hired as the Facilities Maintenance, Grounds & Fleet Manager at Gonzaga.

Spink said that heavy-duty steel and composite laminate were used to construct the area of the MAC that the Kennel Club occupies to better handle the stress of 1,200 students jumping and pounding on the retractable seating section. Despite those preventative measures, according to Spink, the University has to regularly inspect the KC sections and spends $20,000 to $40,000 every two or three years to make repairs and replace fasteners and seats that are worn or have been damaged.

I think most GU players will tell you that it is money well spent.

THE BIRTH OF THE MODERN KENNEL CLUB

In Kyle Kupers' first year as Kennel Club President (1998-99), he literally went door-to-door in the residence halls to get students to officially join the KC and pay their $20 T-shirt fee. He secured 31 paying members.

Kupers ('01) estimates the Kennel Club had most of its members at every game, and says the group know when to cheer and when to jeer—and that they did so well enough to get the entire student section to follow their lead. One thing fans seemed to love was watching the KC leaders diving on the floor for the traditional Kennel Club spell-out, punctuated by a long run and belly flop that brought out laughs, if not a little pain. He adds, "In two consecutive games while spelling Z-A-G-S on the floor, guys busted open their chins or foreheads, and 'Steve-O' (Steve DeLong, Gonzaga's longtime athletic trainer) ended up having to clean it up before the game could start back up."

Kupers recalls watching the 1999 WCC Tournament championship game on ESPN at 723 E. Sharp—a common hangout for the basketball team and friends, where Eric "Big Ed" Edelstein lived with GU players Ryan Floyd and Mike Nilson, as well as a few other students. After the Zags beat Santa Clara for the conference tournament title (on SCU's home court, no less), to earn their second-ever trip to the NCAA tournament, Kupers thought he would head to campus to check out what was going on. A good portion of the student body had the same idea, and a crowd had quickly formed near the Crosby Student Center to celebrate the big victory.

A couple of students approached Kupers with the idea to throw a party right there and then, so he organized a group to get a couple of kegs while he found a place for everyone to gather. At that moment, campus security officers arrived. One of them was a person Kupers had a good relationship with, so he asked if there was anywhere on campus the officers would allow the students to hold an impromptu party. The officer said that they'd stay away from Lake Arthur for the night as long as Kupers kept the group in order. In about 20 minutes, the majority of the group celebrating in front of Crosby had made their way down to Lake Arthur when the kegs showed up. The cold temperatures of March kept the group relatively subdued, but the evening was highlighted when a redshirt freshman on the basketball team who didn't make the road trip to Santa Clara showed up and performed keg stands.

The 1999 2000 season was the beginning of a new chapter for the Kennel Club. After the Zags' remarkable Elite Eight run the season before, students he didn't even know began approaching Kupers for membership in the Kennel Club. The KC budget (revenue from T-shirt sales) went from $620 the year prior to more than $6,600.

Membership in the Kennel Club had grown so much that they started filling one whole section of the student's side in Martin Centre. While it was great to have increased student involvement, it was also a challenge during the early games, because a good number of the newer members had become fans after watching the tournament the year before, but hadn't really participated at the home games. It didn't help that all through the 1999-00 season the Zags were crushing teams at home—most of the games were over in the first half, so the Kennel Club hadn't really been fired up all year. Chants of "Up-by-20" and then 30, and then 40, even 50, were fairly common. Another KC chant would use the opposing team's school name and instead of "University," insert "High School" (e.g., "Santa Clara High School"). One game was such a blow-out, the KC made it through "High School," "Junior High," "Grade School," and "Pre-School" chants, each with significant time in between. But generally, there was a bit of a learning curve as the group went from a couple of dozen Kennel Clubbers to a couple hundred KC members.

On February 3rd, 2000, the Zags played their then-top rival Pepperdine in The Kennel, and according to Kupers, things changed. The Zags came out flat in the first half and promptly fell behind by 15 points. The Kennel went silent. With the team down 13 points with 12 minutes to play, the Kennel Club found its voice and for the first time that season really made its presence felt. The KC veterans took the lead and the new members followed. The last 12 minutes are seared into Kupers' memory, not only because of the excellent basketball being played, but because this new, much larger group was cutting their teeth. The Kennel Club was again rocking.

FOR THE GUYS IN MY ERA that were part of the group who started this thing going, you can ask each and every one of them which gym is louder, and I would guarantee you, hands down, everyone says [the Martin Centre].

Dan Dickau
WCC Player of the Year (2002)
First Team, AP All-American (2002)

"Where before you had a small group of intensely passionate and loyal fans, now you had a whole University living and dying with every shot. It stands as my single favorite memory from Gonzaga basketball and my proudest moment as a member of the Kennel Club," said Kupers.

Over those final 12 minutes, the Zags went on a 25-7 run against a Pepperdine team that would win the WCC regular season title (The Zags finished second that year—and it would be the last time they didn't win the WCC title for more than a decade).

As the team began inching closer to Pepperdine, senior Axel Dench, a KC favorite, dunked with about five minutes left in the game and the Martin Centre erupted. "We were a great team that year, but had come out really slowly and were still down with about five minutes to go in the game," Dench recalls. He hit a three-point shot a few minutes later and the place went nuts again before hitting the nail-in-the-coffin: a banked three that Dench admits was "wholly unintentional." After that final 3-pointer, The Kennel, as Kupers put it, "shared a total out-of-body experience." According to Kupers, this is the moment the modern Kennel Club was born.

"I've got a copy of the game tape and when that ball went in, the crowd, led by the Kennel Club, was so loud and jumping so hard that the camera started shuddering," noted Dench.

Former NBA player and then-Waves coach Jan van Breda Kolff singled out the "hostile crowd" in his postgame interview with *The Spokesman-Review*, noting that the Kennel Club gave the Zags momentum when they needed it most. Dench agreed, "That type of response by the Kennel Club would have had any opposing team begging for the game to be over and done with."

That Pepperdine team was good enough to get an at-large bid to the 2000 NCAA Tournament after losing the conference tournament title game to the Zags, and the Waves would go on to beat Indiana, 77-57, in a first round match-up that would turn out to be Bobby Knight's last game as head coach of the Hoosiers.

Dench, who went to training camp with multiple NBA teams before playing for nearly two decades in Europe and his native Australia, recalled the Kennel Club's impact on games: "I lived on East Mission near St. Al's Grade School, and on my way to games I would walk past the house where the Kennel Club's pregame festivities would be well underway. It was this season where I got to witness the work they'd put into their own game prep. The KC would research the players on the opposing teams, and if any of them had dubious histories or had done anything that would be best kept out of the public eye, the KC would do whatever they could to call attention to it when the players were being announced. Needless to say, the opposing players under the spotlight never had good games after their welcome to the floor."

One story Dench recalled was of Ali Thomas, a guard for the University of San Francisco. He was named the WCC's Newcomer of the Year following his freshman season (1997-98), and was a constant target of the Kennel Club as much for his performance on the court as for his antics and appearance.

Unfortunately for Thomas, he was starting to experience a little bit of male pattern baldness. Now, this was a talented and consistent player, who had some "swag" to him. It started in pregame warmups and continued well after the opening tip, only further fueling the Kennel Club fire. Making matters worse, the Dons came into The Kennel riding a 12-game winning streak, their only loss being a season opening road game versus a Maryland team that would finish second in the Atlantic Coast Conference (ACC)—traditionally known as the top college basketball conference.

So this was a big game, and Thomas strutted onto the Martin Centre floor for warmups with bravado oozing through his sneakers. When his name was announced as part of the USF starting lineup, and he jogged onto the court amidst teammates' high fives, Kennel Clubbers pulled packets of Rogaine® out and threw them onto the court. When Thomas got to the end of the line of his teammates, he was welcomed by dozens of packets at his feet. He wasn't a big player to begin with, just over 6-foot and about 175 pounds, but, as Dench said, "you could see him shrink with the realization that he was going to be the Kennel Club's target all night long."

Dench was indeed right; a player who was a consistent scorer for four years and known to be aggressive (he was among the league leaders in 3-point attempts all four of his seasons), Thomas made only 2-of-7 shots on his way to just 6 points.

Despite losing starter and WCC Defensive Player of the Year Mike Nilson to a season-ending Achilles injury, the Zags won the WCC Tournament title for the second straight year, and the Kennel Club's enthusiasm again played a role. 2000 WCC Tournament MVP Casey Calvary, who would go on to be named Player of the Year in the conference the next year, credited the win to the Kennel Club and the excitement that the group brought with them. "Put their picture in the paper," he told *The Spokesman-Review*, "They deserve as much credit for this as we do."

For several years, the Kennel Club and cheerleaders ushered the team off the court after home games in the Martin Centre. Among the crowd here, 2003-04 KC Co-President, Mike Wall, waits behind event staff for the departing players (backwards visor, shirtless with "A" painted on chest).

After starring for Gonzaga, Axel Dench played professionally in Australia's National Basketball League for the Wollongong Hawks and Melbourne Tigers.

He has also had a varied acting career. He and his son Xavier visit the costume he wore as Wookiee Chieftain Merumeru in Star Wars: Episode III Revenge of the Sith.

Matt Bouldin fondly recalls The Tunnel, a longtime ritual in which the KC formed a human tunnel for the starting five to run through during player introductions. "My most vivid memory of the Kennel Club" says the 2010 WCC Player of the Year, "would most likely be my first start against UW my freshman year, when they called my name and I was able to run through the students on the floor at player introductions for the first time. There is truly no feeling like that when the students and the team become one for that period of time. Over time developing handshakes and other connections with each of the KC members you'd run by really made it special.

Above left: "Alumnus" Bing Crosby donated $700,000 towards construction of the Crosby Library, which was dedicated on November 3, 1957. A bronze statue of Bing was commissioned and placed in front of Crosby Library in 1982. In 1992, Crosby Library became the Crosby Student Center and now houses several student support offices. The Bing Crosby statue is regularly adorned with a Kennel Club shirt.

Above right: The KC has always been creative with its costuming. The 2003 Pepperdine game was a chance for them to get in touch with their inner Elvis. Left to right: Future GSBA President Colin Terry with three "Elvi": Dave Christiansen, Matt Ross, Andy Henning.

THE "BIG ED" SHOW

   The Kennel Club's antics weren't always confined to the Martin Centre gym. Before launching a successful acting career, Eric "Big Ed" Edelstein ('00) got his start in "showbiz" working for GUTV as a student broadcaster for men's basketball games, then turning his talents into performing stand-up comedy at clubs and bars around Spokane. Part of his stand-up routine involved impersonations, and he became a huge success, eventually securing regular gigs on Spokane radio shows before deciding to give Hollywood a try after graduation.

   If he wasn't broadcasting the game, Eric's comedic talent was on full display in the stands at both basketball and baseball games. In fact, Loyola Marymount's baseball coach got so frustrated with Big Ed's heckling that he protested to the umpire, leading then-Zag baseball coach Steve Hertz to ask Eric to tone it down some mid-game. Unfortunately for other visiting coaches, they didn't always have a referee or umpire to complain to about Eric's humor.

   While Spokane is the second most populated city in the state, it isn't all that large, so figuring out where visiting teams were staying was a manageable task. Eric would confirm where visiting teams were spending the night through his connections or just simply by calling the three or four places where teams were most likely to stay. After a few adult beverages, and with an audience of students that would include Kennel Clubbers and, at times, GU basketball players, Big Ed would give visiting coaches a call—you know, just to say hello—and his comedic abilities would take over. Sometimes he would be scheduled to interview the same coach he was pranking the next day for GUTV, so he'd have to remember to disguise his voice and not to laugh and accidentally drop a hint at the joke.

Some visiting players and coaches took Eric's phone calls in stride and would just hang up and, if Eric called back, they'd take their phone off the hook. But a few would react strongly, which only gave Big Ed more incentive to continue the calls.

The University of San Diego head coach at the time was Brad Holland, a former NBA player who was recruited by legendary coach John Wooden at UCLA. As you might guess if you ever saw his intensity on the sideline, Holland had a rather severe reaction to Big Ed's calls.

The night before a game when San Diego was visiting Gonzaga, Eric called Holland's hotel room and started speaking in the voice of Holland's fellow UCLA alumnus Bill Walton, and actually got the coach to bite.

The conversation started off normally enough, but, as Big Ed started taking liberties with what you can imagine Bill Walton might actually say, Holland finally caught on, spewing some expletives before hanging up. Later that evening, after Eric and his audience thought Coach Holland might be back to sleep, Eric called back, and when Holland picked up, Big Ed started the conversation about where the other one left off: "...and another thing, Brad, Coach Wooden would be embarrassed...the plays we would run at UCLA, where is the beauty of an entry pass to Keith Wilkes or the effortless screens and movement to get players like Gail Goodrich open? We see none of that with your team. It's terrible."

This time, after some choice words, Holland took the phone off the hook.

Apparently, he forgot to take his phone off the hook when the Toreros returned to Spokane the following year, though. Looking to relive the humor of the call the year before, Big Ed gave Coach Holland a call again, but this time the coach was prepared, answering the 3 a.m. call with "All right, it's YOU again, huh?"

Eric "Big Ed" Edelstein ('00) is now a professional comedian and actor. His appearances include the 2015 movie *Jurassic World* as well as TV shows such as *Twin Peaks*, *Brooklyn Nine-Nine*, *Parks and Recreation*, *Curb Your Enthusiasm*, *Ugly Betty*, *Drunk History* and *Modern Family*. He is also the voice of the character Grizzly on *We Bare Bears*.

It's totally spontaneous. There are some people who would like us to control what they say[...]. You can't try to teach someone to be free-thinking and then try to manage what they say in a public venue.

Assistant Athletic Director Chris Standiford
Signum (2000)

GROWING PAINS

Although the Kennel Club has grown to become a huge part of the student experience at Gonzaga, it's ascension from the "painted face crew" to a student group officially recognized and working with the University was not without hiccups. Even from the early days, the pregame parties and student conduct at games were not unanimously welcomed by the Gonzaga administration, or even GU alumni and fans. Some saw the group as out of hand. Others, including Dan Fitzgerald, were more steadfast supporters.

At the time the Kennel Club was formed, the legal drinking age in Washington was 21. Yet, 20 miles away, several bars just across the state line in Idaho allowed students to drink at 19. Fitzgerald made the point that, "Kids would just get plowed and drive back [from Idaho]. I said, 'Better here than there.'"

Still, others did not appreciate the raucous support and biting humor of the Kennel Club. After an article by *The Spokesman-Review* reporter John Blanchette in January of 1987 (see reprint on pages 38 and 39) talked up the Kennel Club and its effect on the game environment, some called the University to complain about the sometimes edgy antics. A letter to the editor printed in *The Spokesman-Review* critiqued the Kennel Club as needing to learn more discipline. Something had to give.

Despite the concerns raised by a few, the popularity of the Kennel Club continued to grow. Fitzgerald and others noted the positive effect the Kennel Club had, arguing that it provided a great opportunity for kids to have good fun and a teachable moment should they sometimes get out of hand. A *Sports Illustrated* article spoke positively of the atmosphere in The Kennel, where the Zags had won 145 of its last 183 home games, and the positive press offered beneficial publicity and marketing for a University that was, at the time, struggling with enrollment. Although such publicity is commonplace today, Gonzaga University in the 1990s was rarely a topic of national conversation, so the publicity was invaluable. Positive PR aside, conflict between the Kennel Club and the administration was on the rise.

Aaron Hill ('01, '02), who worked in various capacities in GU Athletics from 1997 to 2006—ranging from student manager for the '99 Elite Eight team to Director of Marketing & Corporate Development, which included being Kennel Club advisor or "liaison"— saw the issue from both sides. Hill's role as team manager had kept him from being an official Kennel Club participant at the men's games as an undergraduate, but two of his best friends were his Jack & Dan's co-workers and roommates at various times in college, Kyle Kupers and Stephen Churney. Both Kupers and Churney would eventually serve as Kennel Club Presidents, so they would always sign Hill up for the KC—"I always bought a membership as an undergrad so that I could get a T-shirt and attend the parties whenever I could," Hill said.

> **THE ARE PLACES** you're supposed to be quiet, like at a golf tournament or at a Sunday morning mass, or at a wake. As long as what they do in the Kennel Club isn't racial or sexual, it's part of the ticket to a Division I-A basketball game as far as I'm concerned.
>
> Dan Fitzgerald
> *GU Athletic Director and Head Basketball Coach*
> The Inlander (1994)

In his role as the Athletics department liaison to the Kennel Club, Hill was only a couple of years removed from attending parties with the students who were now juniors and seniors, and he knew a few of them reasonably well. The role was a bit of tight rope for him. "Admittedly, I did not have much experience managing others, and I had mixed emotions, too," Hill said. "Most of the fans and administration at Gonzaga loved the energy the Kennel

Club provided, myself included. And I knew from working in men's basketball that it was important to the players and coaches. The last thing I wanted was in any way to diminish the energy in The Kennel."

The raucous crowd and energy not only helped the Zags win ball games, but it also helped Hill with marketing and selling sponsorships. "Most of the sponsors loved the Kennel Club," Hill recounts. "But at the same time, the University was worried about making sure nothing embarrassing happened," noting that issues were raised at WCC league meetings, with some of the other schools pushing for GU to rein in the KC.

Various incidents set the stage. Late in the 1997-98 season, the Zags were battling Pepperdine for the regular season title and top seed in the WCC Tournament. Pepperdine had been a traditional power in the WCC, but when coach Tom Asbury left for Kansas State after the 1993-94 season, new coach Tony Fuller could not sustain the success and the Waves hired UCLA assistant coach Lorenzo Romar two years later. Zag fans may most remember Romar from his time at the University of Washington and his cancelling of the annual series with the Zags after the 2006-07 season before restarting in 2015-16.

Romar recruited some high-profile transfers to help rebuild the Waves, including former high school All-Americans Omm'A Givens (who played high school basketball in Aberdeen, Washington, before first attending UCLA) and Jelani Gardner (from Cal), as well as David Lalazarian (Notre Dame) and Nick Sheppard (LSU). Tommie Prince was another transfer to Pepperdine. A prized recruit out of high school who Romar helped steer to UCLA, Prince had his SAT score invalidated and, ultimately, UCLA refused to admit him to school. He went to Arizona State, where he had some criminal charges brought against him (eventually dismissed) before reconnecting with Romar and transferring to Pepperdine.

The Kennel Club had done its homework, and jabs were made in reference to Prince's test scores and criminal charges. The game was neck and neck, with Pepperdine eventually pulling out a win on a late basket. Prince ran towards the Kennel Club and made comments that triggered a couple of KC members to chase him onto the court; one student even made his way into the Waves' dressing room in the Martin Centre.

The GU administration was not amused. The KC members involved got banned for the remaining games and administrators from Gonzaga's Student Life Office gave the KC leaders a stern warning before the next game, threatening to disband the Kennel

Club if anything remotely similar happened again. Kyle Kupers recalls the severity of the message: "I think we were pretty close to getting closed down at that point." But, with only a Senior Night game against Loyola Marymount left on the home schedule, and a few of the KC members banned from attendance, the Kennel Club was allowed to continue.

A similarly close game in the 2004 WCC Tournament, a season which saw the Zags go undefeated in conference play only to be "rewarded" with a tournament game against Santa Clara on their home floor, was another moment that generated some attention from the administration. The WCC Tournament had for years coincided with Gonzaga's spring break, and Kennel Clubbers had recently begun attending the event in larger numbers. Some students temporarily camped out on the tennis court of the team hotel in Santa Clara before the hotel staff figured things out.

Hill was still serving in his role as liaison at this time. ("The term still sounds funny to me to this day—calling me a 'liaison,'" Hill said.) With the game being at Santa Clara's Leavey Center, there was concern something might happen between the Kennel Club and Santa Clara's student group, The Rough Riders, so Hill was assigned to work with the KC to make sure there were no issues. When a late basket in front of where the Kennel Club was seated in the end zone secured a semifinal victory for the Zags, the KC rushed onto the floor to celebrate with the team. "I don't remember much happening in the way of problems," Hill said, "but there was some minimal jawing back forth with Santa Clara's students. To be honest, I didn't think much of it, but league administrators did."

At the annual WCC Marketing Directors' meeting after the season, where all schools would come together to discuss conference-related issues, the Kennel Club was a topic of discussion. "I'm guessing, by how much it was discussed in the lowly Marketing Directors' meeting, that it was discussed at the Presidents' and Athletic Directors' meeting too," Hill surmised. As it turns out, the concerns would lead to other meetings and a pretty dramatic change in the oversight of the Kennel Club by GU's Student Life division.

At the bottom of this [trademark] issue is alcohol use by underage Gonzaga students attending Kennel Club parties at Kennel Club houses, wearing Kennel Club shirts, drinking alcohol paid for by Kennel Club dues. This is a matter of risk management by prudent administrators of Gonzaga University.

Michael Casey
Corporate Counsel, Gonzaga University
The Gonzaga Bulletin *(2004)*

THE GONZAGA UNIVERSITY KENNEL CLUB™

The spring of 2004 was not a good time for the Kennel Club to garner negative publicity. Although KC antics at games that raised eyebrows were pretty rare at Gonzaga during his tenure, Aaron Hill notes that off-the-court issues were causing concern, and things came to a head at the end of that 2004 season.

Rumors started to circulate that the Kennel Club leadership was stockpiling significant amounts of money and some of the leaders were paying personal expenses, such as tuition and rent, out of Kennel Club dues and T-shirt sales (which by that time had expanded from club members only to include sales to fans). One rumor that persisted was that there was a Kennel Club account at a local bank with a balance approaching $80,000. "Whether the rumor is true or not, I have no idea, but the administration was concerned with Kennel Club dues being used to throw off-campus parties," notes Hill, "although more general questions were raised about where the profits were going." And in light of a couple of alcohol-related issues, including liability and negligence concerns arising from injuries from falls from dorm balconies, the University was taking a bit more hands-on approach in combating alcohol use on campus.

After the 2004 season, a meeting was called, and Hill recalls that at the meeting he was told the University was going to appoint a formal advisor to help rein in Kennel Club behavior, the message being there had been several incidents and complaints, and it was necessary to protect the University from lawsuits. And as part of that process, the University was trademarking the name "Gonzaga University Kennel Club" to ensure they controlled usage, such as on T-shirts.

"The University Counsel was there, as were a few other Vice Presidents and members of Student Life who expressed concern about turning a blind eye to students throwing parties and the potential fallout if an accident were to occur," says Hill. "That made a lot of sense, even though I was concerned, as I assume my bosses (in Athletics) were, that University involvement would become a negative and threaten student excitement at games." David Lindsay, who was Director of Student Activities after a long career at nearby North Idaho College, was assigned to be the Kennel Club's co-advisor with Hill. "Let me tell you, David was great, he had experience dealing with students that I certainly didn't have, and he also seemed to get that we had to balance trying to guide them with letting them have fun," Hill said.

"Understandably, the student leaders at the time were not real pleased with some of the changes that would be implemented," Hill went on to say. One change was that money from Kennel Club shirt sales and memberships would be required to be channeled through the University instead of being controlled by KC leadership. "There was even a movement by students to start a new group, 'The G-Unit,' but it didn't really catch on, in part because David [Lindsay] was so good at working directly with students and helping them see the benefits of working together."

This wasn't the first time the logo had been an issue. Former KC President Kyle Kupers recalls being told with certainty that the Club could not use the University's name or logo on T-shirts for 1998-99, so a friend of his created a design without the bulldog in a sailor's cap that the KC had used since its creation in 1984. After Kupers's experience in 1998, a few years later the Kennel Club was allowed to us the University's name and logos. This time, however, in the mid-2000s, there would be no reversal in course. The University was going to control the name, logo and club funds—including money generated from the sale of sponsorship of the Kennel Club shirt.

Hill noted, "At the end of the day, David Lindsay and I thought one way to work with the students was to continue giving a few KC leaders early access to the gym so they could reserve the first row of seats and to try to work with them in a proactive and friendly manner. Hopefully, we thought, we'd develop a good relationship and students would be open to working with us on other issues."

GU Athletics even paid for a few Kennel Club leaders to attend a game in Las Vegas as a show of goodwill, and Lindsay and Hill were sent along as advisors. Kennel Club funds were also redirected to buy pizza for students waiting in line for tickets. About this same time, the University legal team applied to trademark the "Gonzaga University Kennel Club," protecting printing and usage rights, which ultimately ensured control over the T-shirt money from the students. After some of the initial animosity, Hill thought the partnership seemed to flourish. "I remember David being very honest and just awesome— he laid out the case to the students that the best idea was to cooperate, use this as a great resume and experience builder, etc. After that, things seemed to go pretty well. David's leadership in the transition from completely student run, off-the-books organization to cooperation and partnership with the University cannot go unstated."

> **THE KENNEL CLUB is not like any other club … Part of the magic is the informal structure. Part of the problem is the informal structure.**
>
> David Lindsay
> *Former Kennel Club Advisor*
> The Gonzaga Bulletin (2008)

The partnership hit another snag early on, however. For years, the Kennel Club had been selling advertising on the back and sleeves of the KC shirts to fund its activities. Concerns with where the money was going were assuaged with the University helping direct the revenue to things like pizza for students. With construction underway on the McCarthey Athletic Center and sponsorship revenue part of the funding equation, Hill recalls, "There was concern from a major sponsor that their value would be undercut by students selling the back of KC shirts to a competitor. I know I was scared too; it was my job to sell sponsorships, and it was unchartered territory going from basically a handful of loyal companies in the Martin Centre to a full array of corporate sponsorship options in the MAC."

Unwilling to risk losing sponsors whose contributions were necessary for funding the new arena, the Athletics department approached

Northern Quest Resort & Casino, which agreed to sponsor the KC's "Official Sixth Man" T-shirts and things seemed to go well for the opening season in the MAC.

But a year later, in the second season at the McCarthey Athletic Center (2005-06 season), a chant referencing the movie *Brokeback Mountain* implied that a visiting player was homosexual rightfully drew wide scorn and was even picked up by the Associated Press. Articles in *The Gonzaga Bulletin* at the time make it clear the issue was widely discussed on campus. Hill remembers the incident well: "David Lindsay and I found ourselves in another meeting with University administrators and faculty, and a few of them were pretty angry." Lindsay and Hill thought it a good idea to issue a statement challenging GU students to raise the bar.

"From my standpoint, and I was really following David's lead, it was a major teachable moment ... 'Hey, we made big a mistake here, we are better than this, let's not let it happen again.' Thankfully, students agreed, and we started holding weekly meetings with Kennel Club leaders."

The KC Board released an open letter to the Gonzaga Community:

We implore the students of the Kennel Club to show the nation this weekend what makes Gonzaga different. We challenge the students of the Kennel Club to exhibit the class, the creativeness and the competitive drive that has become a foundation of this great university.

An excerpt from a statement issued by University officials to the Kennel Club in response to a chant that received some unwanted national attention.

We, the Kennel Club Board, would like to respond to the recent chanting at our home games. After every home game the Kennel Board tries to understand our weaknesses and strengths as leaders of our club. One of these weaknesses is the ability to control the vulgar language and obscene chants directed towards opposing players. We recognize that the cheers we yell at opposing players not only fall upon their ears, but upon the ears of the faculty, staff, alumni and devoted fans across the nation. We as a group have worked diligently to spread the word that discriminatory chants are not welcome at our school and do not accurately reflect the views of our students. While we understand that it is difficult to manage 1,200 students who are enthralled and engaged in the intense atmosphere of Gonzaga basketball games, we strive to prevent inappropriate cheers from happening beforehand as well as ending them as soon as they start.

Gonzaga University strives to embody equality and appreciate diversity. We, as the Kennel Club, seek to uphold these same values and allow our nation to understand what being a ZAG truly embodies. Although recent events have not accurately represented the desire to uphold these values, the members have shown a strong desire to improve in this area and we are confident that the Kennel Club will be able to demonstrate how intelligent, intense, and respectful we can be.

Sincerely,
Kennel Club Board

Ultimately, having advisors and holding regular student meetings set the stage for the establishment of a formal Kennel Club Board as a means to have more people involved and help set the tone for other students. Hill stressed that he does not want it to be construed that he endorsed what was said in the regrettable KC chant, but he is among the vast majority of people who have done something in their youth who later looked back and said, "I wish I would have handled that better. I know I am thankful things like social media and camera phones didn't exist when I was in college, as I wouldn't want evidence of some of the mistakes I made permanently online." But from Hill's perspective, the growth in the number of leaders was a positive, as more people took ownership for what was, and still is, a huge part of Gonzaga life.

Although Hill left Gonzaga after a few years as Kennel Club co-advisor, Lindsay remained in the position for about a decade. The club grew to 2,500 paying members with an advisory board of 15-20 students. In an interview with *The Spokesman-Review*, Lindsay stated "We are managing a big, volatile situation. You want people to say, 'Man, that was crazy.' You want crazy, but you don't want it to go over the line. Where is that line? It's not a solid line." Lindsay continued to note his job was to serve as an educator. "When you are 19 years old and you are in an event, jumping up and down with thousands of your friends and it's a very intense situation and it's going crazy, it's easy to forget where the line of respect is," Lindsay said. "Humans at this age are pre-programmed to explore. 'What happens if we do this?' Our job is to pad the box so it doesn't hurt so badly when they hit the other end. [...] We have bright students," Lindsay said, "but they are 18- and 19-year-olds in an adrenaline-infused atmosphere. They make mistakes. But as far as the entire Kennel Club going off, that's not been a huge occurrence that we have had to deal with."

Certainly, as in the early days, the Kennel Club is not perfect (what group of any size is?), nor is it for everyone. Detractors remain. But if Kennel Club participation (about 2,000 members, a bit less than half of Gonzaga's undergrad population), attendance and game environment are evidence, the partnership with the University and expanded Kennel Club Board arrangement seems to work. Hill was there at a pivotal time in the transition, and from his perspective David Lindsay deserves great credit. "Making the transition work belongs to David and a few key leaders—Jon Love, Mike Wall, Seth Urruty, and Ryan Franklin among them—who ultimately helped make working with the University a positive experience. It was a tough situation. At the time, I heard a lot of complaints about the University taking over the Kennel Club, but with all the legal ramifications of turning a blind eye, let alone students and parents complaining about how club funds were being used, something had to be done. I think David and whoever in Athletics has worked with him deserves a ton of praise for allowing students to still create the atmosphere the Kennel Club is known for while also being proactive to prevent problems."

Hill states that the credit goes to the students, too, for continuing to find ways to make the Kennel Club a key element of "The Gonzaga Experience," even if the University keeps a bit of a tighter control on things than in the early years.

While the Kennel Club was going through a period of evolution and becoming a more formal, and regulated, organization within the instituition, the basic raw passion remained. The club has long been known for its clever signs, including this classic from the match-up against University of Washington on December 9, 2006.

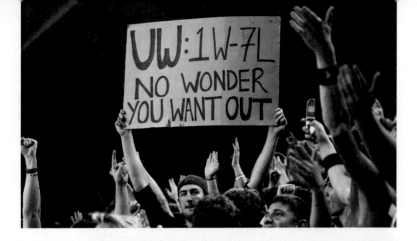

In a much-loved television ad called "We're all on the same team here," the KC cruises campus to celebrate the accomplishments of all kinds of Zags. Here they cheer on Taio Miller ('03), center in sweatshirt after she identifies zagaspore in her microscope. Then-KC Co-President Steve Churney ('02) narrated the video and appears just left of Spike the Bulldog.

David Lindsay, longtime advisor for the Kennel Club, speaking at GU first-year orientation.

Some of the Zags responsible for the bronze bulldog after the GU game against Santa Clara, January 7, 2012.

L-R Steve Robinson ('78), Ian Wehmeyer ('06), Lindsey (Wehmeyer) Weidenbach ('07), Ryan Franklin ('05), Meredith Wehmeyer, Tanna Franklin.

74

The reach of the KC goes beyond the Martin Centre and the MAC, and extends to every generation of Gonzaga alumni.

Steve Robinson ('78)
Chair, Gonzaga University Board of Regents

NEW TRADITIONS

While oversight of the Kennel Club had largely shifted from the students to the GU administration, new KC Co-Presidents Ryan Franklin ('05) and Seth Urruty ('05) realized that the real value of the group was in its ability to bring the student body together in a way that could not be manufactured. Franklin credits the KC with creating a "sense of community" that he doesn't believe he would have experienced otherwise. The Kennel Club gives every student involved some commonality, regardless of their academic class or where they live. "Where else would a freshman who lives in Catherine-Monica get to know a senior who lives off-campus?" Franklin asked.

Despite all the changes, Urruty considers himself very fortunate to have been at GU during that time. "Between the growth of the basketball program and the growth of the campus, our class got to see the transition of the 'old' Gonzaga into the 'new' Gonzaga," Urruty said. This was still a time when it wasn't uncommon for basketball players and regular students to live together. In fact, one of Urruty's and Franklin's housemates was three-time all-conference player, Cory Violette.

Among the many changes to the campus was completion of the McCarthey Athletic Center. While the MAC was still under construction, the Kennel Clubbers decided they needed to be a part of a historic first in the new building. So they put a portable basketball hoop into the back of Mike Davies' ('04) truck and took it down to the construction site. They positioned the hoop where they estimated the basket stanchion would be located, and Kevin O'Brien ('04) made what is believed to be the first basket in the new arena.

The most visible commonality among Kennel Clubbers is the KC shirt. There was a period in the mid-to-late 1990s when the University wanted to distance itself from the KC through the removal of both the University name and the GU Athletics logo that had been used on the KC shirts since 1984. With the trademarking of the Kennel Club name, the University did an about-face and required that the KC shirt bear its name.

Franklin had worked for GU men's basketball since his freshman year. Mark Few approached his former student manager with the opportunity to have Nike design and produce the KC shirts. When Franklin saw the initial proofs from the Nike design team, he thought they were too sterile. He said they lacked the "rawness" of student designs from previous years, and that they didn't capture the KC spirit. Instead of using the Nike design, Urruty created the shirt on his home computer. While he used the University's name as required, it is in the smallest readable type size (See the KC Shirt gallery, pages 151-153).

Another factor in the shirt design was the sponsor. The previous year, 2003-04, George Gee Automotive had been the KC shirt sponsor, but Franklin and Urruty were told that the KC shirt sponsor also had to be a corporate sponsor in the newly-opened McCarthey Athletic Center; anyone wearing a KC shirt bearing a "non-approved" sponsor would not be allowed into the building for a game. Ultimately, Northern Quest Resort & Casino voiced interest and stepped in to help the KC as T-shirt sponsor, a position they have maintained ever since.

According to Phil Haugen, Chief Operating Officer of the Kalispel Tribal Economic Authority (which owns and operates Northern Quest Resort & Casino), the decision to sponsor the KC has been a good one. "The Zags have been an important part of the fabric of our community for decades, and the Kalispel Tribe loves partnering with and giving back to the community," he said. Part of the decision, Haugen noted, was the T-shirts: "Northern Quest has been honored to sponsor the Kennel Club for the past 15 years, providing creative T-shirts that thousands of GU students have proudly worn over the years, bringing a true visual sense of unity to the loudest, most inspirational student cheering section in all of college basketball."

In 2004, sales and distribution of the KC shirts took place off-campus on a Saturday. The KC shirt was sold for $10. The group was not set up to accept any method of payment other than cash, and they quickly realized how that would limit sales. So they began accepting checks made payable to "Mac Daddy's." At the end of the day, they had a shoe box filled with cash and checks totaling more than $20,000. As his housemates at 812 Nora headed out for an evening of partying, Franklin stayed home to protect the club's funds.

The next week, Adam Stewart ('05) and Ian Weymeyer ('06)—who would become KC President the following year—went to a bank and opened a business account under the name "Mac Daddy's" so that they could deposit the funds Franklin had dutifully protected.

One of the challenges Franklin and Urruty faced was the formation of an alternative to the Kennel Club called "The G-Unit." The founders of The G-Unit were students who didn't want to see the social aspect of the KC die, and they didn't want to be a part of the Kennel Club, which now fell largely under University control. After meeting with the group, Franklin and Urruty were able to convince them that they shared the same concerns, and that they were going to find a way to keep the social aspect of the KC alive while working with the University and Athletics. So, along with the KC shirts, Franklin and Urruty sold "6th Man Club" key chains for $20. The key chain gave students 21 and older access to KC events at local bars and other venues. One of those outside events was a concert by Ten Mile Tide at Northern Lights (No-Li) Brewing.

Because Franklin knew the basketball coaches from his days as a student manager, they would sometimes give him insights into how they thought the KC could best impact the game. One example is when assistant coach Leon Rice approached Franklin prior to the game between Gonzaga and the University of

> **I REMEMBER HOW OUR** student section's heckling would get under opposing players' skin, especially in the biggest games. An example was when we had some of those epic in-state rivalry battles with UW: The Kennel Club turned [Husky player] Mike Jensen into a complete mess.
>
> David Pendergraft
> *All-WCC First Team* (2008)

Washington. "Don't say anything to Nate Robinson," Rice said. "He feeds off it ... Ignore him. Pick on anybody else, but we don't want to light a fire under Nate."

Additional insight was provided to the Kennel Club by GU alumnus Steve Robinson ('78), a Seattle attorney who offered to scour public records in search of any indiscretions made by members of the UW team. This led to some creative KC chants about UW players like Mike Jensen.

Nate Robinson led UW with 22 points, but the unranked Zags went on to beat the #14 Huskies, 99-87, for their seventh straight win over their in-state rivals.

Franklin also tells of a game when USF came to Spokane with a player who had been on academic probation. Franklin brought with him a dry-erase board which he used to "quiz" the player with questions such as: "2 + 2 = ?" or "What is the capital of California?" Franklin says the player was a good sport and actually answered each question as he jogged by the KC Co-President's front row seat during warmups.

At the 2004 WCC Tournament hosted by Santa Clara University, Franklin and Urruty reconnected with Robinson and fellow GU alumnus Russell Bevan ('88), a highly-regarded California winemaker. After the Zags defeated St. Mary's in the title game, 84-71, Robinson and Bevan made a run to a local grocery store and purchased every remaining case from the beer cooler. The bounty was a large enough haul to require the use of two of the Santa Clara Marriott's luggage racks to transport it from their car to the hotel lobby, where they proceeded to hand out beers to GU alumni, family, friends and fans.

Terrance Johnson—a Pepperdine player who had been WCC Freshman of the Year in 2002—was so impressed with the camaraderie among GU fans that he told Urruty and Franklin, "This is so cool you are doing this ... I ought to transfer."

Later that year, Bevan invited Franklin to a dinner at the Jundt Art Museum hosted by Dean of the School of Business, Clarence "Bud" Barnes. The dinner was for high-end donors, but Bevan thought that Franklin was a good representative for the type of graduates the school produced, so he invited him to attend. Although Franklin admits to being "way out over my skis," he made a presentation to the group after being introduced by Bevan. Franklin was asked by a donor what he thought was needed at GU, and although he hadn't given it a lot of thought, he said that he felt that the Kennel Club needed a tradition—like rubbing Howard's Rock at Clemson or tapping the "Play Like A Champion

Today" sign at Notre Dame. Franklin suggested a bronze bulldog, like the Testudo the Turtle at the University of Maryland. He thought a bronze bulldog outside the MAC that the Kennel Club could rub before entering a game would give the KC that tradition.

Before leaving the dinner, Franklin had three donor commitments of $10,000 each toward the statue. After consulting with Spokane sculptor Vincent DeFelice, the project cost was estimated at $100,000. The funds remaining in the Kennel Club account at the end of the 2005 school year were earmarked for the bronze bulldog. A plaque at the base of the bulldog acknowledges the contributions of the Class of 2006.

To this day, Franklin and Urruty remain friends with Robinson and Bevan—fellow Gonzaga alumni whose graduation dates are separated by an average of 20 years. In fact, Franklin, Ian Wehmeyer and Andy Bucher ('05) helped Robinson's wife put on a surprise party for his 60th birthday on a GU game night. Where else but Gonzaga would you have Millennials who are friends of a fellow alum from the Baby Boomer generation? As Robinson attests, "the reach of the Kennel Club goes beyond the Martin Centre and the MAC, and extends to every generation of Gonzaga alumni."

Franklin and Urruty have another KC legacy: Tent City. It was a humble start, but what it fostered is anything but humble. The site was on the south side of the Martin Centre under the over-hang above the entry doors. The group had two tents, couches and a TV connected to an Xbox. They camped out twice that season; one of those games was against then-conference rival Pepperdine. The evening before the game, the Waves had a shoot-around at the Martin Centre, and Pepperdine head coach Paul Westphal noticed the group camping outside the building and came out to talk with them. By the end of the conversation, Westphal had invited the group inside to stay warm and to watch his team work-out—the same team he knew the KC would be heckling the next night.

The following year (2005-06), the number of tents had grown to 10 on the west end of Mulligan Field. Today, Kennel Club Tent City regularly houses the occupants of more than 150 tents; the population of Tent City swelled to more than 180 tents when the Arizona Wildcats came to town in 2015.

The site of Tent City has been relocated over the years to accommodate its growth. After a few years on Mulligan Field, it was moved to Herak Lawn or Foley Lawn. But it's much more complicated than just setting up a tent outside the gym as the first Kennel Clubbers did when they camped outside the Martin Centre.

Now it's a process: the first step is to get a game ticket. Ticket distribution usually takes place on the Sunday before a Thursday/ Saturday game. The first 1,200 Kennel Clubbers with valid student identification receive a ticket.

The second step is to get a numbered spot in Tent City. The KC leadership announces a location where sequential tent site numbers will be distributed. Currently, the KC utilizes Twitter for the Tent City announcement; usually around 12pm on the Wednesday prior to a Saturday game. The KC Board goes to great lengths to ensure that no one gets the jump on the rest of the Kennel Club for the numbered tent spots that determine the order in which KC members queue up for the best seats at the biggest games. Groups of students who intend to tent together will spread out over campus in the hope of having one of their "tent mates" get to the tweeted location first.

2017-18 KC President Claire Murphy says that she has been offered "bribes" of food, chocolate, and even cash in return for inside information as to the tent number distribution site. Murphy said that the KC Board now shuts off the location services on their phones two hours in advance of the official tweet, and even check their bags after the boyfriend of a KC Board member placed his cell phone in his girlfriend's backpack so that he could track her location.

Former KC Board Vice President Dave Soto ('12) recalls that during his senior year a fake KC Board Twitter account surfaced. Immediately after the official Tent City location tweet went out, the bogus account sent out a similar tweet directing misled Kennel Clubbers to a different location. Coincidentally, Kennel Clubbers who followed the fake tweet were directed to the site where Soto had been assigned as an official decoy. The unsuspecting Soto then had to deal with angry KC members who had been duped by the fake tweet.

Once assigned a spot in Tent City, each tent becomes the home to up to six Kennel Clubbers starting on Wednesday or Friday, depending on the day of the game. At least one of those six people must be in the tent at all times. The KC Board conducts "tent checks" every couple of hours through the night. If no one listed for that tent is in the area at the time of the tent check, those tent occupants lose their spot in line.

Of course, KC members take this process seriously. Think for a moment about this announcement on the official club blog in 2014:

It's that time of year again Zags! That time when we all willingly leave the comfort of our rooms to go sleep in tents in weather that is clearly too cold, just to establish seats for a single basketball game. Some would call us crazy, yet we are nationally recognized for being dedicated fans and willing to sleep out to see our beloved Bulldogs in their biggest games! It's just one part of what makes us THE BEST STUDENT SECTION IN THE COUNTRY!

Every effort is made to keep the residents of Tent City both warm and occupied. Coach Few has helped deliver food and hot coffee; breakfast burritos and hot chocolate from the Alumni Association have also become a tradition. GU players regularly deliver food to their fellow students to thank them for their support. Aside from food and warm drinks, Kennel Clubbers have found other ways of making their temporary homes comfortable. Tents range in size from backpacking tents designed for a single occupant, to 15-man tents that include all the comforts of home, from futons and heaters to TVs and video game systems. Kennel Clubbers have transformed their tents into a place to have fun and, for some, study.

Impromptu dance parties have led to crowd-surfing tents, and rather than complain about the cold, Kennel Clubbers embrace it with snowball fights.

Two hours before the MAC's Kennel Club doors open—which is 90 minutes before tip-off—Tent City residents can pack up their tents and get ready for the game.

There are other schools that have students camp out for seats, but few do it like the Kennel Club does.

SOUT

The atmosphere here is awesome and the crowd is crazy. The Kennel Club gets so loud and they're definitely our sixth man. No other school has anything close to the Kennel Club.

Adam Morrison
National Association of Basketball Coaches
Co-Player of the Year (2006)
The Gonzaga Bulletin (2004)

IT'S GAMEDAY!

On Saturday, February 11, 2006, the Kennel Club was the featured player in ESPN's *College GameDay* telecast. The GameDay crew of Rece Davis, Jay Bilas and Coach Digger Phelps were amazed at the enthusiasm the KC could generate as a back-drop to a show that was being broadcast live beginning at 9 a.m. Eastern (that's 6 a.m. in the Pacific time zone!). Taking into account that the featured game between #5 Gonzaga and Stanford didn't begin until 6 p.m. that evening, the effort is even more impressive.

The show's producers only gave the Kennel Club two directives: 1) Be in the MAC and ready to go one hour before the start of the broadcast and 2) Be LOUD. For members of the KC, as is the case for most college students, the latter was a lot easier than the former. However tired the KC may have been, the GameDay crew repeatedly mentioned how loud, relentless, and supportive their performance was, especially under the circumstances: Many Kennel Clubbers had begun camping out the previous Sunday to get tickets and the best seats to the game. Joe Tomascheski ('07), then a junior who would become the KC Co-President the following year, estimates that there were 70-80 tents on Mulligan Field that week.

"We camped out on Mulligan Field; the field between the COG and The Kennel. This was before there was field turf on Mulligan, so it was basically a huge frozen mud bowl all winter. The pathways from Catherine/Monica [residence hall] cutting diagonal across the field had to be left clear of any tents so students could still take the shortcut across the field to class," Tomascheski remembers.

However cold it may have been outside the MAC, the Kennel Club and Digger Phelps created some heat inside; Phelps danced with the GU cheerleaders to the music blaring from the MAC's sound system during commercial breaks, and the former Notre Dame coach interacted with the students and signed autographs using his ever-present highlighter that was always color-matched with his tie.

In honor of Adam Morrison, the Kennel Club purchased and distributed 1,500 fake mustaches for the game. The ESPN analyst for that evening's game broadcast was none other than Dick Vitale. Apparently a couple of KC members looked to make the most of the opportunity of getting up close with the inimitable Dickie V; so close that they tried to create a toupee out of fake moustaches for the follically-challenged broadcaster.

The long day (and week, for those camping) ended on a high when the Zags walked away with an 80-76 win over the Cardinal.

At the end of the 2005-06 season, Gonzaga hosted the WCC Tournament for the first time in conference history. While the Zags' #1 seed had been secured by virtue of a 14-0 conference record, Loyola Marymount's #2 seed came as a result of winning a tiebreaker with St. Mary's, after both ended the season with identical 8-6 league marks.

After a harrowing 96-92 overtime win over #5 seed San Diego in the semifinals, the top-seeded Zags seemed primed to claim their third straight conference tournament title—and seventh in the previous eight years—when they faced #2 seed Loyola Marymount on GU's home floor with the Kennel Club in full force.

However, the Lions gave the Zags all they wanted in a game that came down to the wire. After trailing by as many as 15 points in the second half, the Zags put on a surge capped by a J.P. Bautista tip-in of an Adam Morrison miss with one minute to go. LMU's Chris Ayer missed a lay-in at the buzzer to give GU a 68-67 win and the tourney title. It was the Zags' 18th consecutive win of the season and 40th straight home win—both tops in Division I college basketball at the time.

ESPN.com's game summary included the note that "fans picked Morrison up and carried him after the game. Morrison said he felt safe up there."

"'Whoever dropped me would get killed in Spokane,' Morrison said."

One of those who picked up Morrison was Joe Tomascheski.

After the missed lay-in happened at the MAC's west-end basket, the Kennel Club —which had been relegated to two sections behind the east-end basket—erupted. Tomascheski turned his back to celebrate with his fellow Kennel Clubbers behind him when the cheering suddenly increased. He turned back toward the court to see Morrison running toward him, and then jump toward the KC as if to crowd surf. Tomascheski and another KC member grabbed Morrison and lifted him on their shoulders to the cheers of the sold-out MAC crowd.

After the game, several LMU players attended the Kennel Club's postgame party at 811½ Mission. Despite their disappointment over the lost opportunity to beat the #4 team in the country, snap the nation's longest home court winning streak, and secure the WCC's automatic bid into the NCAA Tournament, they praised the Kennel Club for its research and creativity.

Early the next morning, Tomascheski received a text from his mother that read, "Check *The Washington Post*, you're on the front page!" Sure enough, *The Washington Post* had picked up *The Spokesman-Review*'s photo of Morrison being lifted by Tomascheski with a sea of Kennel Clubbers in the background.

The Zags rode the momentum of their undefeated conference season and WCC tourney win into the 2006 NCAA Tournament. After advancing through the first weekend with wins over Xavier and Indiana, the #3 seeded Zags moved onto Oakland for a Sweet Sixteen match-up with #2 seed UCLA. The Zags led by as much as 17 points before relinquishing the lead and the game to the Bruins.

Many believe that was the most talented team GU had ever had up to that point. Had they gotten by the Bruins, they would have had a west coast rematch with #1 seed Memphis—whom the Zags had lost to on the Tigers' home floor earlier that season—for the right to advance to the Final Four.

As brutal as what happened on the floor against the Bruins was for Zag fans, what happened in the stands was equally bad. Tomascheski says that UCLA fans taunted them, threw half-empty water bottles and crumpled cups at them, and even spit on them during the course of the game.

Following the game, Tomascheski and Max Malotky ('07)—who had been Tomascheski's schoolmate since kindergarten and would be his KC Co-President the following year—adjusted their travel schedules to immediately return to Spokane. It must have been a long, quiet, painful flight home.

Fortunately, the 2006-07 season started out with a bang. After wins over Rice and Baylor in the Preseason NIT, the Zags advanced to the semifinal round of the tournament held at New York's famed Madison Square Garden. There, the unranked Zags faced #2 North Carolina, led by All-American Tyler Hansbrough. Derek Raivio paced GU with 21 points and center Josh Heytvelt had a career day with 19 points, eight rebounds and four blocked shots, as the Zags won 82-74. However, the Zag run ended when the other Bulldogs—Butler—defeated GU, 79-71, in the tournament's championship game.

After their strong showing in the Preseason NIT, the Zags made their way into the Top 25 rankings for the first time that season, and were positioned at #22 entering the Hall of Fame Challenge in Phoenix, where they were pitted against a University of Texas squad led by freshman Kevin Durant. The Zags walked away with an impressive 87-77 win over the Longhorns and moved up to #18 in the polls the following week.

> [THE KENNEL CLUB] got us really pumped up and we had to try to calm down. They threw the first punch.
>
> Justin Dentmon
> *Washington point guard*
> Seattle Post-Intelligencer (2006)

The Zags then returned home to face in-state rivals Washington State and Washington. After a disappointing 10-point loss to the Cougars in Pullman, the Zags (and the Kennel Club) got geared up for the #13 Huskies.

The game on December 9, 2006, marked the end of the GU-UW series agreement, and UW coach Lorenzo Romar had announced that the Huskies were not going to renew the series so they could play a more "national schedule," which was a not-so-subtle way of saying that he wanted to improve the UW schedule by playing teams other than GU during the non-conference season. The Huskies had lost seven of the eight most recent match-ups between the two schools, so Gonzaga fans took Romar's announcement as raising the white flag without admitting defeat.

KC Co-President Joe Tomascheski remembers it was the "best energy" in the MAC that he felt in his four years in the Kennel Club.

The *Seattle Post-Intelligencer* tried to describe the scene in the MAC: "Kennel Club members practically exploded when a pounding beat started booming over the public-address system, with [Zombie Nation] signaling a total outburst. The students were an intimidating sight, furiously bouncing up and down while humming to the music. The intensity was impossible to ignore, with both teams coming out and playing at a hyperventilating pitch."

Before the game even began, the Kennel Club put the research it had become famous for to work. Several KC members were graduates of Seattle Prep, the same private school UW freshman center Spencer Hawes had attended. They were aware that Hawes and his girlfriend had broken up during high school, and created the chant: "Lindsey dumped you!"

As Hawes explained to the *Seattle Post-Intelligencer*, "Prep is a pipeline to Gonzaga. (The break-up) was true two years ago. They've got enough snitches."

"They really hammered on Spencer," UW freshman forward Quincy Pondexter said. "It's tough to drown out. You have to just listen to your favorite song in your head."

The KC investigation of the Huskies roster also unearthed junior guard Ryan Appleby's idolization of "Pistol" Pete Maravich; they reminded him that "You're no Pistol!"

There were KC members without shirts who together had written out "LETS GO DOGS" on their chests and "ROMAR'S A CHICKEN" on their backs. Others formed the message "KENNEL CLUB OWNS UDUB" across the front and "WHAT ABOUT NEXT YEAR?" on their backs.

Things only got worse for the Huskies once the game started. The opening tip resulted in an alley-oop dunk by Heyvelt and the KC erupted. Kennel Club chants of "We've got Heytvelt!" "Up by 20!" and "Go home, Huskies!" were heard throughout the game, along with a sign that read "UW: 1W-7L NO WONDER YOU WANT OUT."

By the time a Pierre Marie Altidor-Cespedes dunk sent the crowd into another frenzy, the Huskies had had enough—of both the Zags on the court and the Kennel Club just off it. The resulting 97-77 drubbing was a fitting send-off for the UW toward its "national schedule."

Two weeks later, the Zags would find themselves back at Madison Square Garden (MSG) to face another ACC opponent, this time it was 6th ranked Duke. Despite a game-high 21 points from Jeremy Pargo, the Zags ended up on the wrong end of the 61-54 final score.

Following the game, Tomascheski and a group of Kennel Clubbers, including GU redshirt walk-on Andrew Sorenson, ended up at a bar not far from MSG. They soon realized that former Duke player and then-Chicago Bulls guard Chris Duhon was approaching them. Duhon was in New York with his Bulls' teammates for their game the following day with the Knicks. He had noticed the group's Gonzaga gear and had, apparently, mistaken Sorenson for GU guard Derek Raivio (they were similar in size and did have similar buzz cuts).

When Duhon offered to buy the group a round of tequila shots, "Derek Raivio" and the Kennel Clubbers gladly accepted. Although Duhon repeatedly referred to Sorenson as "Raivio," complimenting him on his "crazy handles" and being a "great shooter," the KC crew didn't correct Duhon because they wanted the free rounds to keep coming.

Unfortunately for them, after a short while, Duhon went and sat with another group at the bar. That didn't stop the KC boys from putting another round of drinks on Duhon's tab. As the former Dukie was cashing out his bar bill at the end of the evening, he seemed to notice that the group from Gonzaga had taken advantage of his generosity. Duhon looked up and gave them a wry smile and a knowing nod. Tomascheski described it as a "you got me" look. Duhon paid the bill and left.

The Blue Devils may have won the game at MSG, but the Kennel Club won the battle at the bar.

Above: Hundreds of students camp out for the Zags' biggest home matchups. First, a KC tweet launches a race around campus to find a secret spot where numbered spots in line are distributed.

Above: ESPN's signature college basketball show, College GameDay, made its first visit to Gonzaga in February 2006, and the Kennel Club made sure to turn out in strength, complete with fake moustaches to honor All-American Adam Morrison. Dick Vitale and Brad Nessler made sure to join in the fun.

Right: In his national media debut, Kennel Club President Joe Tomascheski (bottom right) helps lift Gonzaga forward Adam Morrison after Morrison jumped into the stands following the Zags' 68-67 win over Loyola Marymount in the WCC Tournament title game played at the McCarthey Athletic Center on March 6, 2006. This Spokesman-Review photo was picked up by Associated Press and appeared on the front page of the Washington Post the following day.

*Message painted on the chests
and backs of Kennel Clubbers*

THE PROPOSAL

Shamus O'Doherty ('07, '10) and Breanne Rolando ('07) were storybook high-school sweethearts: He was the quarterback of the Gonzaga Prep football team, and she was the captain of the drill team and a cheerleader at Spokane's Lewis & Clark High School. After graduation, Breanne chose to attend the University of Washington while Shamus went to Gonzaga.

After her first year at UW, Breanne transferred to GU, where she and Shamus were both active Kennel Club members.

Late in their senior year, Shamus decided he would propose to Breanne, but he wanted to do it in a unique and creative way. As he sat at the Jundt Art Museum performing his work-study duties as a "glorified security guard," he decided that he wanted the proposal to take place at McCarthey Athletic Center (MAC) where he and Breanne had shared so many great memories, and where the Zags had yet to lose a game during their years at GU.

His elaborate scheme included having game-specific "messages" painted on the chests and backs of fellow Kennel Clubbers, then at the chosen moment, to re-arrange the letters in those messages to spell out, "MARRY ME BRE." As a KC Board member, Shamus had regular communication with the Athletics department and had planned on the proposal taking place during a pre-arranged timeout at the St. Mary's game on February 10, 2007.

Unfortunately, just a day before the St. Mary's game, he was notified by Athletics that there would be no timeout slots available during the game, and so the proposal date was moved to the Santa Clara game just two days later.

You would think that delaying the proposal by just a few days would not have been a problem, right? Well, it was a problem, a big problem.

See, the "messages" Shamus had come up with were unique to the St. Mary's game; so now he had to start the process from scratch. Quickly, he came up with two new messages related to the Santa Clara game: On the chests of 18 Kennel Clubbers (with "blanks" in between to separate the words) would be "MARK FEW=MR GU" with four unpainted blank chests at the end, and on the backs of those same 18 friends would be the message "DAVEY GREAT CAREER" – referring to the announced retirement of longtime SCU coach Dick Davey.

Again, by re-arranging some select letters in those two messages, with some letters on the chests and others on the backs, you can spell: "MARRY ME BRE." The only letter missing from the two messages was the "B," which Shamus took care of by painting the letter on the chest of his good friend and roommate Nick Franco ('07), and then having Franco wear a shirt until it was time to reveal the secret message.

Along with everything else he had to coordinate, Shamus and his mother, the only family member in on the secret, had secured a half dozen game tickets (a feat by itself) for family: his parents Tim and Sam O'Doherty, his two sisters, Megan ('10) and Erin, and Breanne's parents, Dave and Sue Rolando. In addition, Breanne's younger sister, Olivia, would be in attendance, as she was scheduled to perform with the Lewis & Clark drill team at halftime.

Shamus also planned to sneak his life-long friend Dan Benoit—who was not a GU student, but who Shamus considers a brother—into the KC section using another student's identification card.

While Shamus went about managing the chest and back painting at the Kennel Club's pregame party, one of Breanne's six housemates at East 610 Mission, Kelsey Merwick ('07), was responsible for getting Breanne ready for the big night without making her aware of the surprise that awaited her at the game. Breanne, who had a headache from a long day of classes, wasn't sure she was up for attending the game. It took a little convincing, but Kelsey not only got her to go, but also helped Breanne fix her hair a little to make sure she was ready for what was about to happen.

Although they had gotten to the MAC via separate routes— Shamus with his group of painted Kennel Clubbers and Breanne with Kelsey and a few of her other housemates—they were able to get seats near one another; Shamus stood just one row ahead of Breanne in the student section. At the second TV timeout of the first half (the game was televised on ESPN2), the appointed KC co-conspirators ran onto the court and showed the re-arranged proposal message to the south side (team benches/scorer's table side) of the MAC crowd first. Dan Benoit, who had shaved his head that day to make room for a painted-on question mark, made his way to the end of the line to help spell-out: "MARRY ME BRE?"

Then, with locked arms, the group on the court pivoted to show the north side of the MAC crowd, including the student section. Unaware of exactly what was unfolding on the court in front of him, Shamus' father turned to the person sitting next to him and said, "That's funny, my son's girlfriend's name is Bre!"

As the message rotated into her view, Shamus took a shocked Breanne by the hand and walked her out near mid-court; he then got down on one knee and popped the question. As she said, "Yes," the MAC crowd went crazy. In the emotion of the moment, the Kennel Clubbers who had helped Shamus with the proposal rushed him and carried him off the court, leaving Breanne a few steps behind!

While all of this was happening on the court near the GU bench, Shamus and Breanne's mutual friend, former Kennel Clubber and GU walk-on Andrew Sorenson, was finding it difficult to keep his attention on what was happening in the Zags' huddle during the timeout. Despite the fact that it was a close game, Sorenson sensed the same was true for some of his teammates who were also friends with Shamus and Breanne.

Spoiling the tale's perfect ending, the Broncos beat the Zags, 84-73, for the first GU loss in the four-year history of the MAC and snapping the Zags' 50-game home winning streak, which was the longest in the nation at that time. To this day, former Kennel Club members jokingly blame the loss on Shamus for distracting the team, the Kennel Club, and the MAC crowd with his proposal.

The Kennel Club was well-represented when Shamus and Breanne were married at St. Aloysius Catholic Church on the Gonzaga campus on May 24, 2008. Not only were Kelsey Merwick and former KC Co-President Joe Tomascheski present at the wedding, but they were later married themselves and regularly watch or attend GU games with Shamus and Breanne.

Shamus and Breanne have two children, Addilyn (GU Class of 2034) and Nolan (GU Class of 2037), and Shamus is a partner at the Spokane law firm Randall Danskin.

Shamus says, "I didn't really know what I wanted to do after undergrad, but my senior year was so enjoyable, so awesome, that I didn't want to leave GU." So upon graduating with a bachelor's degree in Accounting, he attended the Gonzaga School of Law and graduated magna cum laude in 2010.

Breanne also graduated magna cum laude with a bachelor's degree in Business Administration in 2007 and is an event planning and public relations consultant.

Shamus' family owns and operates O'Doherty's Irish Grille in downtown Spokane. The pub regularly hosts game watches for the Spokane chapter of the Gonzaga Alumni Association, of which Breanne is a board member, as well as events of the KC Social Club which Shamus laid the groundwork for through his family's connections with local beer distributorships and bar owners.

Multiple Kennel Club Presidents attended the 2000-2001 Men's Basketball Senior Night game. Then KC Co-President Jeff Billows in lower right hand corner. Immediately above him is eventual Co-President Sam Shaw (2001-2002). Next to Shaw holding a Pepsi cup is KC President for 1998-1999 and 1999-2000, Kyle Kupers. 2000-2001 Kennel Club Co-President Scott O'Brien third from the right in front row (backwards hat). 2001-2002 Kennel Club Co-President Steve Churney is over O'Brien's right shoulder (wearing hat, without glasses) while fellow 2001-2002 Co-President Neil Tocher is sixth from the right in first row.

THE DIRT

Jack Quigg had been a Kennel Club member since his freshman year in 2006-07. By the time his senior year rolled around, he had become the KC Co-President along with A.J. Treleven. The biggest opponent on the Zags' out of conference home schedule that year was the ACC's Wake Forest Demon Deacons, who came to the MAC on December 5, 2009.

Back then, the Kennel Club Board regularly put out "the dirt" on incoming teams and individual players in the week leading up to the game to help channel the energy of KC members for the upcoming game. The most intriguing bit of information that their research uncovered that particular week was that Wake Forest player Al-Farouq Aminu, a McDonald's All-American from Nigeria by way of Peachtree Corners, Georgia, had shot a woman with a BB gun at a local shopping center while he was in high school.

Quigg said that the general guideline for KC taunts was that if the player/coach involved had control over the situation, the matter was "fair game." However, if the matter was out of that person's control, it was not to be used against them. The case of Al-Farouq Aminu was clearly an example of the former, not the latter.

So Quigg and his BB gun posse went about creating cardboard cut-outs of the guns that they took with them to the Wake Forest game. They quickly caught the attention of Aminu, then a sophomore, during pregame warmups. His teammates, who obviously knew the story, got a laugh out of it, too.

Just a few days after the 77-75 loss to Wake Forest, the Zags hosted Division II Augustana College from Sioux Falls, South Dakota. Jed Keener, who was on the KC Board as a junior and would become the KC Co-President the following year with Justin Tai, got to the game along with his KC cohorts almost two hours before tip-off—plenty of time to strike up a 'friendship' with the visiting players.

From his front row seat on the eastern end of the KC section, Keener wasted no time in initiating a conversation with Augustana players as they began their pregame warmup activities. Immediately, it became clear to him that Augustana's players were very excited to play a Top 25 team (GU was ranked #21 in that week's poll). They asked Keener what sort of crowd they could expect on a Wednesday night, and when he told them that it would be a sell-out, that seemed to excite them even more.

As the game drew near, Keener asked if he could take a shot from his corner of the court. Without hesitation, an Augustana player passed him the ball and Keener let one fly from deep.... It was no good. So he asked for another try, this time from a little closer, and he knocked it down.

> **WILEY JUST THREW THAT** ball [inbounds] in front of the students and they were all over him, and [… Demetri] Goodson stepped right in there and took the ball away and then gave a nice assist to Steven Gray who was following on the play, so credit the student section on that one.
>
> Craig Ehlo
> *Former NBA Player and TV analyst for the November 18, 2008, game versus Idaho*

With each successive make, the reaction from the Kennel Club and the MAC crowd grew. Finally, on what would be the last of Keener's five or six shots, the flask he had stowed away in his back pocket fell onto the floor and slid all the way to the elbow area of the key. Security had finally seen enough of the sideshow-turned-featured act, and escorted Keener from the building.

Fortunately, Keener had a good relationship with GU Athletics' Marketing Director Matt Beckman, who intervened on his behalf. Beckman assured security that, once separated from his Canadian whiskey, Keener no longer posed a threat to the Augustana players or GU's reputation as a fine Jesuit institution of higher learning, and he was allowed back into the building for the Zags' 79-40 drubbing of the Vikings.

Quigg also worked closely with Beckman. Interestingly, one of Quigg's duties as KC Co-President was to go to the Northern Quest Casino to pick up the check for their sponsorship of the KC T-shirts. The person Quigg and Treleven met with was none other than former GU Athletic Director and head coach, Dan Fitzgerald, who by that time was the casino's Director of Community Relations. Tragically, Fitz would pass away just a few months later.

The 2009-10 season marked the end of the Kennel Club tradition of allowing the incumbent KC President or Co-Presidents to hand-pick their successor(s). Quigg and Treleven selected Jed Keener and Justin Tai to lead the KC in 2010-11, but from that point forward KC Board positions were appointed via an interview and selection process conducted by the Gonzaga Student Body Association (GSBA) under the guidance of Athletics and Student Life. Through this same process, representatives from each class were also selected to serve on the KC Board. The intended outcome was to spread participation in the day-to-day operation of the KC among a broader group and to provide greater transparency to the student body on how membership fees were being managed.

In response to this demand for transparency, Kathryn McGoffin, the first KC President to be selected via this new system, and the KC Board went to great lengths to ensure KC members received value in return for their $25 membership fee. In addition to the KC shirt, the board began distributing other items at games (e.g., snap-back caps); they also created a clear line of demarcation between the KC membership fees and those for the Social Club— which is only open to those 21 and older.

Another advancement was allowing credit card payments for the first time, utilizing the University's internal payment processing CashNet system. The most visible work of the new independently selected KC Board was the design and installation of the graphic on the doors utilized by the Kennel Club to enter the MAC.

This period in Kennel Club history was also highlighted by some of the best teams in the country making their way to The Kennel and experiencing the wrath of the Kennel Club for the first time. In 2011, Michigan State came to town. Led by future NBA All-Star Draymond Green's 34 points, on 11-of-13 shooting from the field and 8-of-9 from the free throw line, the Spartans beat the Zags 74-67 in front of a sold-out MAC crowd, and a rambunctious

Kennel Club. Following the game, Green made his way to the press table—in the middle of the KC section—for a postgame interview with the ESPN broadcast team. When he was done with the interview, Green went over to KC Board Vice President Dave Soto and a few other KC members giving them hugs and high-fives and stating that, "You guys are as good as anybody in the Big Ten." Pretty high praise from an All-American who had played in some of the greatest college basketball venues and in front of some of the most rabid fans in the country.

Soto might be the most recognizable KC member of all-time, due largely to the Zag-style lucha libre (Mexican wrestling) mask he wore to every game. Soto became so recognizable that he was regularly asked to take pictures with GU fans and their children, and was even told that he appeared on someone's Christmas card one year.

McGoffin also attributes the growth of the phrase "Zag Up" to Soto. Although it now appears on everything from flags to coasters, the KC was the first to use the phrase on T-shirts sold to the public. The following three years, the phrase appeared on a sleeve of the KC shirts; and in 2014, in celebration of the Kennel Club's 30th year, the KC made "Zag Up" jerseys available to the public and distributed "Zag Up" socks to its membership. A shot of the Kennel Club and a close-up of those socks were a part of the musical introduction on CBS featuring the band U2 for the 2018 NCAA Tournament. In fact, GU players wore long sleeve shirts bearing the phrase in the tournament in 2018.

In a 2011 article in *The Gonzaga Bulletin,* Soto said, "[The Kennel Club is] a cool way for people to meet each other. I know that a lot of the people that I am friends with now, I met at basketball games. Everyone is there with similar interests." McGoffin believes that those friendships carry over to life after graduation. She says, "Being a part of the Kennel Club is lifelong membership with the Gonzaga community." McGoffin cites as an example of that connection among former Kennel Clubbers the reaction she's witnessed to the playing of Zombie Nation at wedding receptions. "Nothing gets them out on the dance floor like that song," she said. "The camaraderie and school spirit are what unite us, regardless of the class year."

Quigg is now a sales manager for Maxum Petroleum in Seattle; Treleven is part of the fourth generation of leadership of his family's business, Sprague Pest Solutions, based in Tacoma; Keener is a graduate of the Creighton University School of Dentistry and has joined his father's dental practice in Redmond, Oregon;

Soto is a coach and Sports Information Director at Cate School in Carpinteria, California; and McGoffin is a Certified Public Accountant with KMPG in Seattle.

Above: It will be hard to top the marriage proposal to Breanne Rolando that Shamus O'Doherty arranged during the game against Santa Clara on February 12, 2007.

Saint Mary's center Omar Samhan long suffered the KC's wrath when the Gaels came to town. His quality play also helped spur a new and long-running rivalry between the two programs.

Dave Soto and his trademark lucha libre mask among dozens of loud students. Former NBA Player and TV analyst, Craig Ehlo, was on the broadcast for the November 18, 2008, game against Idaho, and pointed out the KC's influence on the game: "[Brandon] Wiley just threw that ball [inbounds] in front of the students and they were all over him, [...] Goodson stepped right in there and took the ball away [...] so credit the student section on that one."

Below: The official Kennel Club entrance on north side of McCarthey Athletic Center.

*Last year, Samhan replied to one especially
inciteful message with a laundry list of all
that is wrong with Gonzaga and Spokane.
When the Gaels came to town, the Kennel Club
responded with chants of "Spo-kane-hates-you."*

East Bay Times *(2010)*

(STILL) THE MOST HATED MAN IN SPOKANE

Hamlet had Claudius; Popeye had Bluto; Harry Potter had Voldemort; Seinfeld had Newman. Every protagonist wearing a white hat in a 1950s Western had to deal with at least one antagonist wearing a black hat acting as his foil. And during the 35-year history of the Kennel Club, no one wore the black hat better than Omar Samhan.

The 6-foot 11-inch, 270lb center for Saint Mary's seemed to enjoy playing the role of the villain and the negative reaction he received from opposing fans around the WCC—especially in Spokane. But unlike hockey goons, whose only assets are physical stature and a willingness to do whatever is necessary to take out the opposing team's most skilled players, Samhan was very skilled himself. He was a Freshman All-America selection by *CollegeInsider.com* in 2006, and he was named WCC Defensive Player of the Year and All-WCC first-team after both his junior and senior seasons. In his final year at Saint Mary's, Samhan led the Gaels to a 28-6 record—including an 81-62 win over Gonzaga in the WCC Tournament title game, after losing to the Zags by a nearly identical score in Spokane a month earlier. The Gaels made their deepest run in school history that year, advancing to the Sweet Sixteen of the 2010 NCAA tournament, where Samhan scored a combined 61 points in SMC's two wins, including 32 points in a victory over the #2 seed, Villanova.

Samhan admits to throwing fuel on the fire of the SMC-GU rivalry by inserting himself into the Zags' huddle during a timeout in a game his freshman year. That game also featured a verbal exchange with Mark Few that included an expletive from Samhan and led to a call by Zag fans for a public apology. Samhan soon became public enemy #1 in Spokane. In a recent article in *The Spokesman-Review*, Samhan stated that, "It was fun for them and me. Back home they ran a huge article, 'The Most Hated Man in Spokane.' I still have it up in my house."

> [THE KENNEL CLUB] always get[s] on me," Samhan said. "I expect them to be how they always are, getting on me and everything else. They always have something special. I love playing in that kind of environment.
>
> Omar Samhan
> *Saint Mary's center*
> East Bay Times (2010)

The fan reaction to Samhan grew worse as his performance on the floor improved and the games between the two teams grew tighter. The Kennel Club bestowed nicknames such as "Ham Sandwich" and dressed in sumo outfits draped with a replica of Samhan's #50 uniform. They even created shirts depicting a bulldog eating a #50 jersey. "The whole crowd had them on," Samhan said in an interview with the *East Bay Times* in 2009. "I have a friend that goes there, had him grab an extra one for me. I gave it to my mom. She wears it like it's cool. I'm like, 'Mom, it's not cool. They're making fun of me.' She says, 'I just like it because it says 50.' I'm like, 'OK, do what you want.'"

The rivalry was so intense that he'd sacrifice benefits for his own school to see the Zags lose. He once acknowledged to *SI.com* that Gonzaga beating Syracuse in the second round of the 2010 NCAA tournament would help the conference, "But I still want them to lose."

Much like the late-night calls from Eric "Big Ed" Edelstein to San Diego coach Brad Holland a decade earlier, Samhan shared that "[Kennel Club members] used to call my hotel room at 3 in the morning. I was so dumb, I'd pick up. And we'd have a conversation! I went to the game and there was a guy in a fat suit yelling, 'I called you!' It was awesome. By senior year, there was this running dialogue on Facebook."

Despite his willingness to interact with the Kennel Club, both on and off the court, Samhan and the Gaels never experienced a win on GU's home floor during his college basketball career (2006-10). In fact, the Gaels won just three of the two teams' ten meetings during that time. Still, that dominance didn't alter the KC's view of their arch nemesis.

Former SMC teammate Mickey McConnell says Samhan "loves being the guy who's hated."

Mission accomplished.

Hey, welcome to the team, man!

J.P. Batista to former Kennel Clubber
Andrew Sorenson

KENNEL CLUB WALK-ONS

For the vast majority of Kennel Club members, their experience with Gonzaga basketball is limited to a few hours a week in the student section at the McCarthey Athletic Center from mid-November to early-March. But for a very lucky few, the experience becomes something beyond cheering in the stands.

Andrew Sorenson was a freshman living in DeSmet Hall in the fall of 2004, when he decided that he didn't want to give up his basketball dream. He had grown up in Olympia, Wasington, watching the Zags, inspired by their Cinderella run through the 1999 NCAA Tournament and attending Gonzaga's summer basketball camps. He had played all the way through high school and had achieved some success playing for the Class 4A Olympia Bears. He was a regular participant in pick-up games at the Martin Centre, so he soon learned of the annual walk-on try-outs where students were provided with the opportunity to show the GU coaches what they could bring to the program if given the chance.

Sorenson was one of six participants at the one-day try-out in mid-October. Coach Tommy Lloyd conducted the work-out with the assistance of a couple of student managers. The prospective walk-ons went through a series of drills that helped Coach Lloyd identify players with potential. Unfortunately for all six walk-on candidates, the coach elected not to take anyone from the group.

However, Coach Lloyd did offer Sorenson the opportunity to be involved with the team—as a manager. After giving it some thought, Sorenson told Coach Lloyd that his "passion was playing" and that he would be back to try-out the following year.

So, Sorenson's "Gonzaga Experience" started simply as a student. Along with many of his friends and dorm mates, he joined the Kennel Club—he still has his KC shirt—and cheered for fellow freshmen David Pendergraft and Josh Heytvelt, sophomores Adam Morrison and Derek Raivio, senior Ronny Turiaf and junior college transfer J.P. Batista as they led the Zags to WCC regular season and tournament titles before losing to Texas Tech, 71-69 in the round of 32 in the 2005 NCAA Tournament.

During his freshman year, Sorenson was a regular in the front row of the Kennel Club section. In fact, his parents sent him a screen shot from an ESPN2 broadcast of a GU game in which Sorenson appeared as the exclamation point in the message of "GONZAGA BULLDOGS!" that he and his friends had painted across the bare chests.

Sorenson also participated in the regular late-game KC call for the then-walk-on darling of the student section (and future GU assistant coach) Brian Michaelson.

The next fall, as the basketball season loomed, Sorenson got an unexpected call on his dorm room phone—it was Coach Lloyd. He called to confirm that Sorenson was planning to try-out again as he had promised. At the end of the brief conversation, Lloyd asked for Sorenson's email address. Within the hour, Sorenson received an email from the coach re-stating when the try-outs would take place.

Sorenson admits that the unexpected call and the follow-up email threw him for a loop. He told himself that he couldn't "let them into [his] head," so he tried to focus on doing the things he could control and "leaving it all out on the floor" at the try-out.

Later that week, Coach Lloyd was joined by former GU player and then-staff member Kyle Bankhead. The two coaches put the walk-on candidates through a similar set of drills as the year before. After the first-day session was over, Lloyd said to Sorenson, "Are you sure you want to do this? You know, this is a really big time commitment." Sorenson assured him that he wanted to continue, to which Lloyd said, "Okay, we'll see you tomorrow."

At the end of the second day's session, Coach Lloyd gathered the 6-8 participants and thanked them for their time. He also complimented them for having the courage to try-out when so many others were too scared or intimidated to do the same.

He offered to help anyone who wanted to pursue their hoop dreams at another school. Hearing that, Sorenson assumed that his Gonzaga hoop dream was over for another year. His thoughts immediately turned to the Business Management Information Systems exam he had the next morning at 8 a.m. Then, Coach Lloyd concluded his remarks to the group by saying, "But we're going to give Andrew a shot."

It wasn't until Chris Pontarolo-Maag—one of Sorenson's fellow walk-on candidates and a future GU walk-on himself—poked him with his elbow and said, "He's talking about you!" that Sorenson realized that Lloyd had just offered him a spot on the team. He was a Zag!

As Lloyd and Sorenson walked off the MAC floor, Lloyd noticed Sorenson's black basketball shoes and said, "We'll have to get you another pair of shoes—Coach [Bill] Grier hates black basketball shoes." Sorenson thought, "Wow! I'm already scoring some cool gear!" That thrill was short-lived, however, when he realized what "Zag Swag" remained for the last guy added to the roster; the only practice gear that was left was an XXL jersey and a similarly huge pair of basketball shorts. The slight 6-foot 2-inch, 170 pound Sorenson recalls: "I looked ridiculous!"

The next day, as he walked onto the floor for his first official practice as a member of the GU basketball team, Sorenson was approached by J.P. Batista. The Brazilian center immediately gave him a bear hug and said, "Hey, welcome to the team, man!"

Not only did Batista share that moment with Sorenson; he also shared his locker. Like practice gear that fit, an open locker was not available for the walk-on, so Batista made space in his locker for his new teammate.

Even though he was now a member of a nationally-prominent college basketball team, Sorenson didn't let that deter him from having a complete student experience as well. He was elected to serve as Vice President of the Knights of Gonzaga (a sophomore men's service organization whose past membership included many of the KC co-founders), and he continued to live on-campus in DeSmet Hall along with many of his closest friends and a roommate, Conor Henderson, who was one of Sorenson's teammates on an intramural basketball team that won a championship his freshman year.

Sorenson was so close with the students that at times he found himself a bit caught between what his friends were doing in the stands and what was happening on the court. For instance, during a timeout while Coach Few was diagramming a play, Sorenson's friend Kenny McKerlick ('08) was one of three students selected to shoot a half-court shot for a prize jackpot as part of a sponsored promotion. As McKerlick's shot sailed through the hoop and the Kennel Club erupted, Sorenson found it difficult to keep his focus on what was going on in the huddle.

It was a balancing act for Sorenson, focusing on the court while being intrigued by what was coming from the Kennel Club. That balancing act could sometimes be difficult for the GU coaching staff as well.

After taking part in the KC call for Brian Michaelson his freshman year, Sorenson was on the receiving end of similar calls during his GU career. Sometimes, in the midst of the persistent calls of "Sor-En-Son! Sor-En-Son!" from the Kennel Club, coaches would glance down toward him at the end of the bench as if to say, "You know, we can't put you in when they call for you or else they'll expect it every game." He understood. Still, it must have been cool hearing 1,200 of his fellow students and closest friends chanting his name.

The Zags advanced to the Sweet Sixteen Sorenson's first year on the team (2005-06), and they were WCC regular season champions all four years he was on the roster. By his senior year, he had been awarded a full scholarship.

On Senior Night in 2009, not only did Andrew Sorenson start the game, but he was named "Player of the Game" with 15 points, including three 3-pointers. Sorenson said that his motto going into that game was, "If I'm open, it's going up!"

"It was an AMAZING night to share with my teammates, coaches, my family, the Kennel Club, the fans, and the whole Zag and Spokane community," he said.

Sorenson is now an Operations Manager at Nike headquarters in Beaverton, Oregon. He was assisted along the way by former Kennel Clubber, GU Trustee, and Nike VP for Global Footwear Sourcing & Manufacturing Greg Bui. Sorenson and Bui are joined at Nike by former KC President Sara Wendland; and GU alumnus John Naekel used to help design the Gonzaga basketball uniforms for Nike. Bui has been at Nike for over 28 years. Mary Roney, a graduate of the GU class of 1984 and a Senior Event Planner at Nike, is the second longest tenured "Nike Zag" with nearly 25 years with the company.

KENNEL CLUBBER FOR A DAY

Though Mike Hart was also a walk-on, his route to the GU roster wasn't nearly as circuitous as Sorenson's. However, like Sorenson,

Hart came to Gonzaga with academics as his priority. He had only received passing interest from the basketball coaches at Pacific University, a Division III school located in Forest Grove, Oregon—less than 30 miles from where Hart had played high school basketball at Jesuit in Portland. Hart was a senior when future GU star Kyle Wiltjer was a freshman at Jesuit.

Prior to arriving on the Gonzaga campus for his freshman year in the fall of 2008, Hart had sent then-GU assistant coach Leon Rice a brief email expressing his interest in the Bulldog program. Rice never returned his message, so Hart went about starting his academic career at GU without the thought of becoming a student-athlete. Once he arrived at GU, however, Hart became quick friends with GU players and DeSmet Hall dorm mates Andy Poling, Grant Gibbs and Demetri Goodson. While playing intramural sports with Hart, the players quickly saw the potential in the 6-foot 6-inch Hart as an athlete. Poling and others talked the GU coaches into allowing Hart to participate in "open gym" scrimmages with team.

Meanwhile, Hart became a Kennel Club member and planned to attend Gonzaga's Midnight Madness event (which eventually evolved into Kraziness in The Kennel). Hart recalls that when he arrived at the event he immediately felt out of his element among the hundreds of students dressed in identical KC shirts. "It wasn't really in my personality to be so excited, so animated," said Hart. Amongst all the exuberance and enthusiasm, Hart found himself a silent observer.

Although he was friends with many Kennel Club members and some of the KC leadership during his years at GU, Hart's Kennel Club participation was limited to that single experience. The next day, he attended the walk-on try-out and was immediately added to the team. He spent his first year on the team as a redshirt, but by his senior year he had secured a scholarship and had become nationally-recognizable as the "glue guy" on a Gonzaga team that was ranked #1 in the nation. Seth Davis of Sports Illustrated and Jeff Goodman of CBS Sports both wrote articles featuring Hart.

Hart was always a favorite among GU fans and the Kennel Club alike for his hustle, defense, rebounding and the intangibles he brought to the Zags. On his Senior Night, as he was being taken out of the game for the last time, nearly every person in the MAC stood and used their hands to form the "Hart" symbol. What a perfect name for a guy with so much heart.

While Hart felt uncomfortable being in the midst of the craziness of the Kennel Club, he felt more at home on college basketball's biggest stage—as a starter on a top-ranked team that was a #1 seed in the 2013 NCAA tournament. Hart said that he finally felt like a true Kennel Clubber when he attended the 2017 NCAA Final Four to watch the Zags take on North Carolina in the championship game. "It was the first time I felt comfortable cheering," he admitted. "Being a member of the Kennel Club requires the same commitment and investment as being a player, just in a different way."

After spending a season as a student assistant to the Gonzaga program, Hart spent a year as a full-time assistant on the basketball staff at Colorado College—a Division III school located in Colorado Springs. He then decided to put the master's degree (MBA) he had earned at Gonzaga to good use and accepted a position with a commercial real estate development and consulting firm in Spokane.

KENNEL CLUB PROGENY

The latest GU player with a Kennel Club link is Jack Beach. He is the son of former GU baseball player and Kennel Club co-founder Dan Beach ('88). He is the first GU basketball player to have a parent who was in the Kennel Club.

Jack Beach was born to be a Zag. He grew up in San Diego playing basketball with his dad and his brother Jeff (an assistant on former GU coach Bill Grier's staff at the University of San Diego) on a sport court imprinted with the GU Bulldog logo. One of Jack's dad's best friends is Bob Finn, who played baseball with Dan Beach at GU and works in the Alumni Association office at Gonzaga. He also happens to be the first-ever Kennel Club President.

Jack Beach played on the prestigious Adidas Gauntlet AAU national circuit with and against multiple 4- and 5-star players bound for Division I schools. His high school career at Torrey Pines (CA) High School culminated in a run to the Southern California CIF sectional semifinals. In that semifinal match-up, Torrey Pines faced Chino Hills, led by Lonzo Ball and his brother LiAngelo. Torrey Pines led the entire game up until the final three minutes when Lonzo Ball took over and demonstrated why he would become an NBA lottery pick by leading Chino Hills to the win while scoring a team-high 28 points. Beach matched Ball's scoring with 28 points to lead Torrey Pines.

Beach received several inquiries from Division I teams, including Creighton, Army and Navy, but deep down Jack knew he wanted to be a Zag, no matter what role he had to take to do it. Ironically, Beach was recruited as a "preferred walk-on" by Gonzaga assistant coach Brian Michaelson, himself a former walk-on at GU.

Jack Beach is one of at least a dozen current GU students or alumni who are the children of Kennel Club co-founders. The others are Torrey Finn (daughter of Bob Finn); former GU baseball player Brendan McClary and Lindsey Peterson (son and stepdaughter of former GU baseball player Shane McClary); Amy, Cara, Megan, and Brad Nickolaus (children of Curt Nickolaus); Kennedy McGahan (daughter of Chris McGahan); Charlie and Emily Shields (son and daughter of Mike Shields); Austin Twiss (son of Bob Twiss) and Payton Zenier (daughter of Jeff Zenier).

I love Gonzaga very, very much. Gonzaga is a special place with special people and I will never forget my four years here.

Ronny Turiaf
Three-time, first team All-WCC
2005 WCC Player of the Year
2018 WCC Hall of Honor Inductee

THE KENNEL CLUB CARES

While some of the Kennel Club's missteps have been widely broadcast, many of its more positive impacts have not. And while the KC has led or participated in community service projects dating back to the pet food drive promoted in *Sports Illustrated* in 1988, what may speak louder is what the club, and individual members of it, have done without any promotion or fanfare.

On several occasions throughout this book, I have used the phrase "The Gonzaga Experience." People from my generation of GU students will recognize that phrase as one used by the University to describe how being a part of the Gonzaga community can change one's life. While all Gonzaga students and alumni have their own, personal "Gonzaga Experience," I want to tell you two stories—one story of individual sacrifice made by one KC member for another, and the other a story of a former player who the Kennel Club supported after his GU playing days were over. Each had a life-changing effect on the people involved and are great examples of how "The Gonzaga Experience" continues long after graduation.

Steve "Brez" Brezniak and Jason Boyd were Kennel Club Co-Presidents in 1990-91. Boyd had also been KC Co-President alongside GU pitcher Billy Walker in 1988-89, and had been a walk-on with the baseball team the following season. Brezniak had participated in a walk-on try-out with the basketball team his freshman year and had not made it. Instead, he was offered a position as "15th man" (student manager), which came with $500 worth of compensation for the entire season. After participating in off-season work-outs with the team in the summer following his freshman year, Steve declined the opportunity to be involved with the team his sophomore year so that he could focus on his studies.

One of the things Steve did to support Jason was formalize the group that consisted largely of basketball players and their friends who attended GU baseball games; a similar group had been attending baseball games since the earliest days of the Kennel Club, and it was Brezniak who named the group the "Hill Crew."

Brezniak's and Boyd's lives continued to cross as they shared many milestone moments together: As luck and the alphabet would have it, they were seated next to each other at their GU graduation in 1991; they lived together in Spokane that summer; in 2003 they attended the BB&T Classic in Washington, DC, which GU won by defeating Maryland and George Washington; they went to spring training together in Arizona; and in 2006, Jason was a member of Steve's wedding party.

In October of 2006, Steve's mother passed away from complications caused by Polycystic Kidney Disease (PKD). She had gone through kidney dialysis for some time before receiving a transplant while Steve was at GU. Steve knew that he had inherited PKD and over the years had jokingly told his friends, "Someday I'll be calling you when I need a kidney."

Little did he know how soon he would need to make that call or how difficult a call it would be to make.

In February 2009, Steve was told his kidneys were failing. Normal kidneys are the size of one's fist; Steve's clogged kidneys were the size of a football. The waiting list for a "cadaver transplant" was more than six years long in California, so his only other option was to find a living donor. After months of testing relatives and friends for a genetic match, including his wife Kim and his pastor, the realization that Steve would soon need to begin regular dialysis and an unknown future hit him.

Despite Steve's prediction that he would someday call his GU friends for help, he was reluctant to do so, and those friends did not know the extent of his situation until Kim posted on Facebook: "We're out of people, and I'm not sure what's going to happen next." Steve's friend, former Kennel Clubber and Editor of *The Gonzaga Bulletin* Mark Briggs, responded to Kim's post with a Facebook post of his own with the subject line of "Brez needs our help."

Within 24 hours, many of his Gonzaga friends, including former GU baseball player and KC President Jim Fitzgerald and Steve's KC Co-President Jason Boyd, had responded to Briggs' post. Steve says of the 14 people who completed the initial screening survey, ten were Gonzaga friends. Boyd's survey was the first submitted and he was found to be a perfect match.

The transplant took place on February 4, 2010. Steve was released from the University of California San Francisco Medical Center on February 7, and Jason was released the following day. The surgeon who performed the transplant called it a "textbook procedure."

Jason lives in Portland with his daughter Keeley. Steve and Kim now live in Temecula, California, along with their son, Grayson, and their twin daughters, Mattea and McKinley.

When Steve and Jason went to the BB&T Classic in 2003, they saw Gonzaga center Ronny Turiaf win the tournament's Most Valuable Player award. After watching the Zags play live for the first time at the 2003 Pete Newell Challenge, Kim Brezniak became such a Turiaf fan that she and Steve would later name their Shih Tzu "Ronny" in honor of him.

Turiaf wasn't only a favorite of Steve and Kim Brezniak; he was a favorite of the Kennel Club and all of Zag Nation. Ronny's personality, the passion with which he played and his love of Gonzaga and Spokane—a place far different from his boyhood home on the small Caribbean island of Martinique—endeared him to Zag fans both young and old.

After his senior season—highlighted by being named the WCC Player of the Year—Turiaf was selected 37th overall in the 2005 NBA Draft by the Los Angeles Lakers. During a physical exam conducted by the Lakers' medical staff less than a month after being drafted, Turiaf was found to have an enlarged aortic root in his heart. His medical condition jeopardized his basketball career and his life.

Earlier that year, a Gonzaga student had sustained a serious injury when a fight broke out at a house party. Although the postgame party was not hosted by the Kennel Club, many KC members were present and wearing their KC shirts (as they would be following a game), so many assumed that it was a Kennel Club function. Eventually, it became clear that the person who caused the injury wasn't a KC member or even a GU student.

A parent of the injured student threatened to sue Gonzaga. Because the Kennel Club was not an official club and, therefore, not sanctioned by the University, the KC leadership was told it needed to "lawyer up."

The KC Board was referred to GU alumnus Steve Robinson (he of Snake Pit and Bronze Bulldog fame) who advised the KC leadership to develop a defense fund in case legal action was taken against them. The KC Board decided to redirect monies previously earmarked for KC social events to the defense fund. Ultimately, the threat of a lawsuit was dropped, and the defense fund was no longer deemed necessary. At that point the KC Board voted to give the balance of the fund to Robinson in compensation for his representation and efforts in resolving the issue. Robinson, however, did not feel comfortable with that arrangement and suggested that the KC Board identify another option for the dissolution of the fund.

Around this time Turiaf's medical condition became public. The Lakers had made it known that they would cover his medical bills, but it was obvious that Turiaf's condition would preclude him from earning a living in the short term. In response to those needs, The Ronny Turiaf Assistance Fund was created. With the help of Robinson and the Athletics department, the KC Board received clearance from the NCAA to contribute the balance of its defense fund to the expenses related to Ronny's surgery and rehabilitation.

Turiaf made an astonishing recovery. Less than six months after his surgery in July of 2005, Ronny made his NBA debut. That fall, in just the second game of the 2006-07 NBA season, he scored a career-high with 23 points (on 8-10 shooting) in the Lakers' 110-98 win over the Golden State Warriors.

Turiaf went on to have a very successful playing career that included an NBA championship with the Miami Heat and appearances with the French national team in the 2006 World Championships and the 2012 Olympic Games in London.

The Kennel Club cares. Indeed.

A Kennel tradition, here from a game in the 1996-97 season: Left to Right: Michael Dolmage, partially obscured; Z – Wayne Bastrup; A – Jason Druffel; G- Ben Peterson; S – Shannon Boroff.

Top Left: After a second try-out, Andrew Sorenson became an early Kennel Clubber to make the transition to walk-on player.

Top Right: Mike Hart only attended one KC event, but ended up a starter for the Zags.

Left: Future GU player and son of KC co-founder Dan Beach, Jack Beach (then age 8), on his "home court" in San Diego with Bob Finn, Gonzaga Alumni Outreach & Engagement Director and first-ever President of the Kennel Club.

The term "walk-on" is used in collegiate athletics to describe an athlete who becomes part of a team without being recruited beforehand or awarded an athletic scholarship. This results in the differentiation between "walk-ons" and "scholarship" athletes.

A "preferred walk-on" is an athlete who is offered a roster spot on the team without having to try-out, but is not provided with a scholarship.

Andrew Sorenson was a walk-on; Jack Beach is a preferred walk-on. Ultimately, Sorenson was awarded a scholarship.

KC co-founder Mike Shields' daughter Emily Shields ('21) and son Charlie Shields ('18) pose in front of one of the six seats at the MAC bearing a name of a Kennel Club co-founder.
(Note: Emily is wearing an original KC shirt from 1984.)

THE KC IS READY FOR ITS CLOSE-UP

While it was often a delicate balancing act between University integrity and some awkward antics by the Kennel Club, the KC was a favorite of those attending the games, young and old alike. After Gonzaga reached the Elite Eight in 1999, and followed up with successive trips to the Sweet Sixteen in 2000 and 2001, the basketball program was being courted for televising its games. "If we're going to be on TV, we'd better have a TV ad or two to help market the University to prospective students and benefactors around the country," thought Dale Goodwin, the University's Public Relations Director by this time.

The third advertisement created—and the first professionally done—featured, appropriately enough, the Kennel Club. Goodwin came up with the theme, "We're all part of the same team here," to remind viewers in the region and around the country that Gonzaga is more than just basketball. It is a community of people who share a common mission and vision, and a love of this highly rigorous academic institution. The thirty-second spot was created by Gonzaga alumnus Frank Swoboda ('94) and his team from Corner Booth Productions.

By this time the Kennel Club had gained national attention, and it seemed appropriate to use one of its Co-Presidents, Steve Churney ('02), as spokesman in the

114

ad. Aboard a Stingray bicycle, Churney leads a group of Kennel Clubbers around campus, high-fiving revered Alumni Chaplain Fr. Tony Lehmann, SJ, and visiting Professor Nancy Staub's biology class to cheer on a student who identified the organism under the microscope as Zagaspore. "These people are the best and the brightest," Churney remarks. Next, the Kennel Clubbers are onto a student's flute recital, and the closing scene pans out to see the Kennel Clubbers cheering wildly for the young lady's effort. The Clubbers are next seen cheering a made layup during men's basketball practice, much to the amazement of Coach Mark Few, who extols: "Hey, give it a break guys. It's only practice," as the cheering dies to a hush. They wake up Lewis in his dorm room and make sure he gets to class on time, and end with a shot of the troupe running to the Engineering building to cheer on those making great accomplishments there. Churney closes with "So much to do, so little time. We're all part of the same team here."

That ad was so well received that the GU public relations team signed on another Kennel Club member, Sean Ryan ('04), to host the next ad.

Ryan takes viewers on another campus tour in which academics, the arts, spirituality, community and support are high points of emphasis. And it starts off with Ryan getting a French lesson from Gonzaga's most notable player at the time, Ronny Turiaf, the two lying on the floor at center court in The Kennel. Action moves to the art studio with students painting still-life images of four gentlemen posing with Z-A-G-S painted across their bare chests, and onto a chemistry lab where a female student in white lab coat stirring a bubbling mixture in a large test tube tells the boys, still with Z-A-G-S across their chests, "I promise this will take off the paint and no more." Cut to the Law School courtroom where Ryan is learning debate, and takes what he learned in the classroom to apply in real life (The Kennel), shouting at the referee "I strongly disagree with that call, Mr. Referee."

It closes with an Erroll Knight dunk in The Kennel, and Ryan exclaiming, "I like to think I'm helping, too. We're all part of the same team here."

These TV ads are two of Gonzaga fan favorites, but not the end of the national publicity for the Kennel Club. *Sports Illustrated* featured Kelly Olynyk surrounded by Kennel Clubbers on the cover of a 2013 issue and, two years later, the KC was again the backdrop when Kyle Wiltjer appeared on the cover of the magazine.

From a simple mention of the Kennel Club in the "Short Shots" section of *Sports Illustrated*'s college basketball report in 1988—in the midst of the Zags' 16-12 season and fifth place finish in the WCAC (WCC)—to Kennel Club members being on the cover of the same magazine with the Zags' top player and future first-round NBA draft choice from the #1 ranked team in the country in 2013, the men's basketball program and Gonzaga University had come an incredibly long way in a relatively short period of time.

And the Kennel Club had been along for the ride the whole time. Former GU player Bryce McPhee may have given the Kennel Club the greatest compliment when he said, "They were Zags."

We're all part of the same team here.

Painted chests have long been on display in the Kennel. Left to Right: G – Michael Hunter ('01); O – Ben Lyman ('01); N – Moses Byrd-Rinck ('01); Z – Mike Wasson ('01); A – Will Hart ('01); G - Randy Teel ('01); A – Andy Cooper ('01).

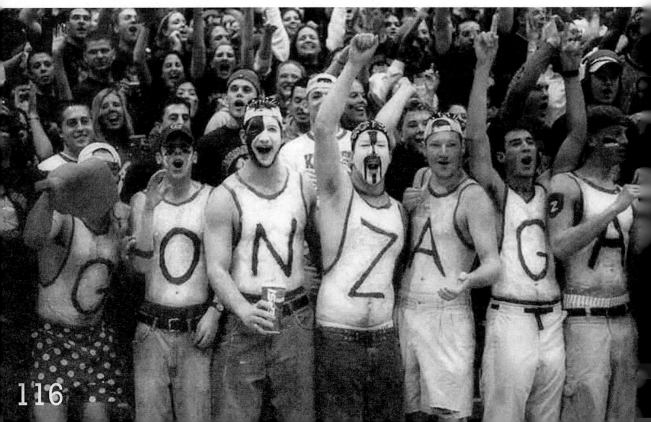

Back in 1984, if someone would have given me million-to-one odds of all this happening, I wouldn't have wasted a dollar.

Bob Twiss ('84)
Kennel Club Co-Founder

THE PROMISED LAND

As far as the Gonzaga basketball program had come when it appeared in the NCAA Tournament for the first time in 1995, and then when they went on the magical Elite Eight run in 1999, the Final Four still seemed a distant dream. Even when the Zags began to consistently advance into the second weekend of the tournament, they just couldn't seem to avoid the heart-breaking loss (Arizona in 2003 and UCLA in 2006), to shut down a hot shooter (Steph Curry in 2008, Jimmer Fredette in 2011 and Wichita State in 2013), or to get past the blue bloods (Michigan State in 2001, North Carolina in 2009 and Duke in 2015).

As the 2016-17 season progressed, it became obvious that this team, this band of brothers who had been recruited out of high school, transferred or walked-on, was something special. They rolled through the regular-season with one blemish, a 79-71 loss to BYU on Senior Night. They swept through the conference tournament and captured the WCC's automatic bid, not that they needed it. They entered the NCAA Tournament as the #1 seed in the West region and immediately took out Mike Daum and South Dakota State by 20 points. They had a bigger challenge with Northwestern, a tournament and media darling, but ultimately held off the Wildcats, 79-73.

The Zags then moved on to San Jose, California, where Jordan Matthews' three-pointer with less than a minute to go pushed GU over the top in a dramatic 61-58 win over a very good West Virginia team in the Sweet Sixteen. They then thundered to a 24-point win over #11 seed Xavier to advance to their first-ever Final Four.

As crazy as things were for GU alumni and Zag Nation, it may have been craziest for the Kennel Clubbers who were in the midst of the resumption of the semester after spring break. They not only had to deal with classes and homework, but they had to figure out how to get to Arizona. The KC Board helped by making $100 travel subsidies available to 200 qualifying members of the KC. For future KC Board Vice President Collin Calhoon ('18), that meant some funds for the more than 20-hour road trip (if you drive straight through) from Spokane to Glendale, Arizona, that he and many of his fellow Kennel Clubbers endured.

Unlike the other student sections represented at the Final Four, the Kennel Club's allotment of 750 game tickets sold out in less than three minutes. Yes, you read that right; less than three minutes! And the only reason it took that long was because the system set up to take the orders couldn't handle the volume of requests any faster. Meanwhile, the NCAA had to recruit students from Arizona State University to fill the seats at each end of the court at University of Phoenix Stadium that had been reserved for North Carolina and South Carolina students.

For Zags who were studying abroad, like future KC Board member Dylan Graff ('18) and future KC President Claire Murphy ('18), the travel subsidy the Kennel Club offered would not have done much good. Graff and Murphy were students in the Gonzaga-in-Florence (GIF) program in Florence, Italy. GIF program participants included about 120 Gonzaga students and another 30 students from "sister" schools like the University of San Francisco, Loyola Marymount, Marquette, St. Joseph's, Seattle University, and the University of Portland. But for that one weekend, at least, all 150 GIF students were Zags—as they all wore Gonzaga gear and many joined in on the face-painting for the Final Four games.

Murphy, who was in Dublin, Ireland, for the semifinal game, found her way to the historic Temple Bar area of the city. As she and Julia Donovan ('18) started looking for a place to watch the game, they spotted a couple in GU apparel walking down Temple Bar Street. As the couple passed, Murphy and Donovan shouted, "Go Zags!" Upon hearing those words, the couple stopped in their tracks and struck up a conversation. Kristin Kleist Schmitt ('08) is a Gonzaga alumna and a former GIF student who was visiting Dublin with her husband, John Schmitt. The Schmitts were heading to a place they were told might be showing the game and invited Murphy and Donovan to join them. When the group arrived, the place turned out to be a night club on the other side of the River Liffey called The Living Room. The club's owners set up a television on the edge of the dance floor at 2 a.m. to allow Murphy, Donovan, the Schmitts and anyone else interested to watch the Zags as they took on South Carolina. Club goers came and went, but by the end of the game, everyone who remained knew how to pronounce "Gonzaga."

Back in Italy, Graff—who had watched the South Carolina game in Copenhagen before flying back to Florence—used his connections with the staff at Uncle Jimmy's, a favorite hang-out in Florence among American tourists and "Gonzaghini," as GIF students were once known, to arrange for the bar to remain open for the 3 a.m. tip-off (local time) of the national championship game. As the tourists and locals shuffled off when the bar officially closed at 2 a.m., some complained that they had to leave while the Gonzaghini were allowed to stay. But bartender and part-owner Karl Thomas quickly retorted, "It's all about the Zags tonight!" Over the course of the next three and a half hours, Uncle Jimmy's became the Florentine version of Jack & Dan's Tavern, with chants of "Go! Gonzaga! G-O-N-Z-A-G-A!" and "Z-A-G-S! Let's go Zags!" filling the bar.

Meanwhile, former team manager and GU Athletics employee, and then-Oklahoma State University professor Aaron Hill was on a week-long business trip to Milan, Italy. "Thankfully, I flew out on the Friday of the second weekend of the tournament, so I was able to watch the games against South Dakota State, Northwestern and West Virginia at home. I streamed the Xavier game Saturday night in my hotel room in Italy. After living in the U.S.'s Central time zone for several years, I was used to watching games late into the evening." Watching the Zags beat Xavier, Hill was in his own version of heaven. "I threw my own little celebration; I had a few drinks in my hotel room just thinking, 'Wow! We finally did it!'"

Hill couldn't believe that after 30-plus years as a fan, including a decade working with the program in various capacities spanning his undergrad years and employment within the GU Athletics department, he was going to miss the Final Four. "I was pretty disappointed I couldn't make it to Glendale. This was a big moment for the program, and a number of my close GU friends were going—even Axel Dench made it all the way from Australia— and here I was, stuck in Italy. I guess I shouldn't complain, but I think it soured me on playing tourist a bit."

Hill's flight back to the U.S. was scheduled for the Sunday between the semifinal and final, and in an attempt to make it to Arizona for the title game, he had devised a plan to jump off his return flight while on a lay-over in Dallas and make a connecting flight to Phoenix. The plan seemed perfect, but it was foiled by a cancelled flight. "We boarded the plane in Milan as scheduled, but sat there for about two hours before they de-planed us with a mechanical failure. We were rescheduled to fly back Monday, and so I changed my flight again. This time the plan was that I'd switch off of my flight, my buddy would pick up my large suitcase in Stillwater (Oklahoma), and I would run to a different flight with one change of clothes in my computer bag and make it to Phoenix. Unfortunately, I narrowly missed the connection in Dallas. Hard to believe it was two different flight delays that kept me from the game, but I am confident they'll be back, and I won't miss it again!"

My personal journey wasn't quite as dramatic as Aaron's, but like him, just being there was very important to me. As the Zags seemingly got better every year, I promised myself that if GU ever broke through and made it to the Final Four I would go—regardless of whether I had game tickets or a place to stay; I just wanted to celebrate with Zag Nation.

However, when GU beat Xavier to qualify for the Final Four, reality set in. Now a middle-aged man, I had become accustomed to the comforts of home, and I wasn't going to travel all the way to Arizona and be in a place where I couldn't share this experience with my closest friends. So I lit up my phone with calls to GU friends I hadn't seen in years, as well as people I had never met—from ticket sources to landlords of Phoenix-area rental properties—all in an effort to fulfill my portion of the promise.

Ultimately, I arranged to rent a house in Glendale. It was perfect. From the front yard of the house, one can see University of Phoenix Stadium in the distance; and the house's 5,500+ square feet of interior space made it a comfortable, temporary home in the desert for 13 of my good friends—including two of my roommates from the house at 624 East Sharp, Sean Hogan and Bob Twiss; and two more from The Baldwin House, Mike Harrington and Joe Roberts.

After the semifinal win over South Carolina, most of the guys headed off to the nearby McFadden's Restaurant & Saloon, which had become our pre- and postgame headquarters. I understood my friends' desire to celebrate, but I could not bring myself to leave my seat at the stadium. As I sat contemplating how far "we"

Though the rowdy days in the old Martin Centre are long past, original Kennel Clubbers – the KCOGs (if you have to ask, check with your kids) – still turn out to most every game, often when the Zags are playing on the road. Left to right, Jeff Zenier, Chris McGahan, and Mike Shields cheer on the Zags. against San Diego in 2004.

The connections between the Gonzaga baseball program and the Kennel Club have always run deep. A chance meeting at Jack & Dan's Tavern provided a reunion for several men with ties to both.

Left to Right,
Dan Beach ('88),
Aaron Hill ('01),
Chris Spring ('87),
Mike Shields ('84),
Mark Machtolf,
Steve Hertz ('72).

Some of the KCOGs at the 2017 NCAA Final Four in Glendale, Arizona.
Front, left to right: Mark Walatka ('84), Michael Easter ('84), Chris McGahan ('87), Mike Shields ('84), Bob Twiss ('84).
Back: Bruce Molina ('90), Paul Kelly ('84), Jeff Zenier ('88), Tim O'Neil ('87), Mike Harrington ('84).

had come, so many memories came rushing back for me. The memory of working at Fitz's basketball camps during the summer after my senior year in high school and getting to meet GU players I idolized, like Tim Wagner and Eddie Taylor; the thrill of watching Father Coughlin being carried around the gym after GU's 79-67 win over conference power USF in 1981; the excitement of seeing the score of a Gonzaga game on ESPN SportsCenter for the first time in 1983 when Dave Clement's put-back beat DePaul, 49-48; the honor of witnessing the beginning of John Stockton's evolution into a Hall of Famer; the hundreds of games I saw in person and the thousands of hours I spent indoctrinating my kids by watching countless televised Gonzaga games with them as they grew up. It was as if I was dreaming; and if I stood up and left my seat, I might wake up and the dream would end; and I didn't want it to end. Ever.

On the day between the semifinal and final, Gonzaga hosted a Sunday service at a downtown hotel. As most of the congregation was leaving, I noticed Dale Goodwin and his family near the front of the room. Dale had been one of the first people I met when I arrived at GU in the summer of 1980, and it was important to me that I connect with him during this special time. As I approached Dale he turned and gave me a hug. I wanted to say something profound to him, but my emotions wouldn't allow me to force out the words. As we stood there, neither of us said anything, but that silence spoke volumes.

During Monday night's championship game, I remember trying to soak it all in. Despite my conscious effort, I can tell you very little about what happened from the opening tip to the disappointing end. I actually had to watch a recording of the game to see the many things I missed live.

I can't imagine how cool it will be WHEN the Zags win it all, because it was just so cool getting there. But WHEN that day finally comes, the Kennel Club, and especially the KCOGs, will be there with them. Just as we have been since 1984.

POSTSCRIPT

One of the things that came out of Aaron Hill's Final Four travel adventure was this book. A few of the people he was working with in Milan were from the University of South Carolina, Gonzaga's semifinal opponent. One of them said to Aaron, "I'm sure glad we don't have to play you in Spokane; I've heard the Kennel Club is unreal." The Gamecocks fan continued that he had been told that the Kennel Club was so good because the GU rugby team had started and led the group. That misconception led Aaron to determine that the real story of the Kennel Club needed to be told. During the Final Four, he reached out to Jeff Zenier to inquire about the KC co-founders' interest in writing a history of the group. As is turns out, "Z" was staying with me and a few other KCOGs in the house I had rented in Glendale. The rest, as they say, is history.

As a result of writing this book together, Aaron and I have become friends. And through the hundreds of emails, texts and phone conversations we've had, we have come to realize our similarities and the many intersections of our lives. For instance, we both grew up in small, rural communities in Eastern Washington (Aaron attended Freeman High School, just outside Spokane; and I grew up near the tiny town of White Swan on the Yakama Indian Reservation); we were both student managers at GU (Aaron with the basketball team, and I was with the baseball team); we were both graduate assistants to Steve Hertz and the Bulldogs baseball program; we both have brothers named Andy (Aaron's brother is an assistant on the basketball staff at the

University of Utah; and my brother graduated from GU in 1996 and worked with Aaron's dad, Rick, at Kimmel Athletic Supply); we were both bartenders at Jack & Dan's; we were both Athletics Marketing Directors at WCC schools (Aaron at GU and I was at the University of Portland); and most amazingly, we both lived next to Sister Antonia (aka, *Our Lady of the Perpetual Yard Sale*) at some point while GU undergrads. I have begun telling people that Aaron and I are identical…with the exceptions that he is younger, smarter, and better-looking.

Aaron's role in writing this book was invaluable. He is so well-connected and so good at maintaining relationships that doors seemed to fly open when he would call. And most importantly, he is the very definition of a "Zag." In my view, that is one of the highest compliments one can be given, and Aaron deserves it as much as anyone I know.

The Kennel Club was ahead of its time.

Jay Hillock
Gonzaga head coach
(1981-85)

TOP "NAMED" BASKETBALL STUDENT SECTIONS

(Listed by date founded)

Illinois: Orange Krush (1975) [1]   33,932 undergrads*
Gonzaga: Kennel Club (1984)   *5,160 undergrads**
Duke: Cameron Crazies (1986) [2]   6,609 undergrads*
Michigan State: Izzone (1995) [3]   39,090 undergrads*
Florida: Rowdy Reptiles (1998) [4]   34,554 undergrads*
San Diego State: The Show (2001) [5]   29,853 undergrads*
Pitt: Oakland Zoo (2001) [6]   19,123 undergrads*
Wisconsin: Grateful Red (2002) [7]   31,710 undergrads*
Kentucky: eRUPPtion Zone (2002) [8]   22,621 undergrads*
Arizona: ZonaZoo (2003) [9]   34,072 undergrads*
Iowa State: Cyclone Alley (2003) [10]   30,671 undergrads*
Virginia: Hoo Crew (2005) [11]   16,331 undergrads*
Utah State: The Hurd (2006) [12]   24,838 undergrads*
Indiana: Crimson Guard (2009) [13]   39,184 undergrads*
Iowa: Hawks Nest (2009) [14]   24,476 undergrads*
Arizona State: 942 Crew (2011) [15]   42,477 undergrads*

The Kennel Club forms "The Tunnel" during introductions at a game in the 1999-2000 season.

WHAT THE PLAYERS SAY

John Stockton (1980-84)

The guys who formed the Kennel Club changed the energy at Gonzaga games. They were boisterous, and it seemed like they were right on top of you. They created a hostile environment for opposing teams; there was nothing like it in the conference or anywhere else we played.

Bryce McPhee (1980-85)

They were the most educated, intelligent trash-talking fans that not only ridiculed players and poor performances without spewing vulgarities, but a few would also dress up and mimic every move of opposing coaches... It drove them all crazy!

Jeff Condill (1983-86)

The Kennel Club brought its energy and unique talents to every game. We relished the home court advantage our friends and classmates gave us.

Jim McPhee (1986-90)

Just like today, the Kennel Club created a fired-up venue. The noise helped our momentum and highlighted every mistake made by opposing teams. Other student bodies made noise, but none were louder and none had the Kennel Club's organization and creativity. That made the Kennel Club better than any other student body.

127

Geoff Goss (1990-94)

One cannot aptly describe the feelings [The Kennel] produces, the excitement it generates, nor the pain it can inflict on the opposing team's psyche. In other words, The Kennel is pure madness wrapped in a gym. The creation is the ultimate college basketball setting which has no equal.

Jeff Brown (1991-94)

The KC is the nation's best student section, and it's not even close! [...] Both Duke and Gonzaga have made the strategic decision to provide the best seats in the arena to students to create an electric atmosphere that has a significant impact on the energy and difficulty of winning a game there.

John Rillie (1992-95)

The comparison between the Kennel Club and other student sections wasn't even close in my day. It was the Kennel Club, then daylight.

Matt Santangelo (1996-2000)

I remember an article in *Sports Illustrated* prior to my commitment. I believe the Kennel Club was ranked in the Top 5 student groups in the country. That was definitely influential in my decision to come to GU.

Richie Frahm (1996-2000)

The old Martin Centre was basically a high school gym, but the Kennel Club made it a special environment. It was the type of environment where you want to play. It's a big part of the 'Gonzaga effect' that other schools crave.

Mike Nilson (1996-2000)

The energy the Kennel Club brings to our team makes Gonzaga the toughest place to play in America. In my experience, there's no comparison. The Kennel Club is the most energetic, crazed group of people I've ever played in front of.

Casey Calvary (1997-2001)

The ferocity of the Kennel Club was a big reason why I signed with Gonzaga. You want to play at a place like GU— with the Kennel Club's preparation, the tunnel, the atmosphere—they'd set the environment and get the rest of the fans going.

Dan Dickau (2000-02)

I was blown away by how loud they were, and how they stood and were engaged the entire game. I still can't believe that there were guys standing next to the referee and yelling in his ears!

Winston Brooks (2001-03)

Playing in The Kennel is something that I wish everyone can experience! The energy that the fans bring to the game is unbelievable and that's why this is one of the hardest places to play in the country!

Richard Fox (2002-04)

I don't think anyone could overstate the impact the Kennel Club had on the game environment, particularly when Gonzaga played in the old Kennel. It felt like the students were on the court and the energy they created in the building was something our teams really fed on.

Ronny Turiaf (2001-05)

Our crowd is crazy. When it gets going, nobody in the nation can play in The Kennel.

Derek Raivio (2003-07)

The Kennel Club provided us with a major home court advantage. During my four years at GU, we played at schools like Virginia, Missouri and Washington—all of which had great student sections—and the Kennel Club blew them out of the water.

J.P. Batista (2004-06)

I just want to say thanks to you guys; I think you guys are the soul of this program... I love you guys, man!

David Pendergraft (2004-08)

The consistent passion the Kennel Club brings is incredible. I can't emphasize enough how much that energy and environment changes your energy level as a player. When the KC is down, the energy of the players usually follows. There is a lot of power in the Kennel Club, more than I think they realize.

Matt Bouldin (2006-10)

Every player I have come across outside of the actual Kennel […] who had played in The Kennel against me or past/recent teams always mentions 'Zombie Nation.' The way it not only intimidated them, but really showed opposing teams the love and admiration the Kennel Club had for basketball. They were jealous of what we got to experience night in and night out.

Kelly Olynyk (2009-13)

"You guys are the best fans in the nation," Olynyk said in a video message on the Jumbotron at Kraziness in the Kennel on October 12, 2013. "Keep that up. Zag up!"

David Stockton (2010-14)

I do not think any student section really compares to the Kennel Club. Not only are they as crazy and as loud as any school in the country, but the connection between GU players and the Kennel Club is unmatched. I knew almost everybody in the KC, and had relationships with them. The community that Gonzaga creates is what makes playing there so special.

Byron Wesley (2014-15)

The [Kennel Club] is phenomenal. Every game—regardless of who the opponent is—they come, and they come ready. It's a real home-court advantage and that's something I'm not used to, and I can only imagine how tough it is for opposing teams to come in here and have to deal with that crowd all night.

Domantas Sabonis (2014-16)

The Kennel Club has the best fans in the country. They're crazy and they get everybody involved. It's a great home court advantage. I miss the Kennel Club!

Kyle Wiltjer (2013-15)

It gets the whole arena rocking and that means, for us, it's definitely an energy boost. Seeing [the Kennel Club] jump up and down, it gets us going.

Zach Collins (2016-17)

There is nothing like playing in The Kennel in front of those fans. When some nights it was tough to 'get up' for games, the Kennel Club gave me energy I didn't think I had. I'll always cherish playing in front of the best fans in the country.

Przemek Karnowski (2012-17)

I've never played in front of a crowd like this, the Kennel Club and a full house every game, it's crazy. Like I said, it's special, I love the fans.

Josh Perkins (2014-18)

From my freshman year until now, I still get the same chill bumps and inner excitement when I walk out onto the floor—and ESPECIALLY when 'Zombie Nation' hits around that four minute mark. I just think that, no matter what, our home crowd sticks with us and at the moments we need them most, they get even louder, providing that spark we sometimes need.

Jack Beach (2017-18)

BYU is always pretty wild, but I would take the Kennel Club over them any day. I remember SMU being pretty loud when we were there because they serve alcohol to the students during the game. I'm pretty excited to go to Chapel Hill this year (2018) and see what North Carolina has to offer, but overall I'm taking the Kennel Club with the first pick in the student section draft.

Corey Kispert (2017-18)

It's hard not to be passionate with the crowd that we have. When they show up and shout like that and are loud like that, we really feed off it. They're a huge part of how much energy we have.

Silas Melson (2014-18)

The Kennel Club is like no other, it's almost like you look into the stands and see a sea of red with all the fans going crazy in their KC shirts.

Johnathan Williams III (2016-18)

I think we have the best fans in the country, in my opinion. I've never played in front of a crowd this crazy, they bring the same energy every single night, day in and day out, and I appreciate that and I love them to death.

Killian Tillie (2016-18)

I love playing here and being a part of the amazing culture at GU. I'm anxious to play another season under great coaches with a great group of teammates. And, I can't forget to mention how great it is to play in front of the Kennel Club and all of our Zag fans.

Richie Frahm runs through "The Tunnel" during a game in the 1997-98 season.

Left to right,
Mark Few,
Dan Monson,
Dan Fitzgerald,
Jerry Krause,
Steve DeLong

WHAT THE COACHES SAY

Jay
HIllock,
Former GU
& LMU
Head Coach

They were, by far, the best student section in the WCC. Their antics were great and they made Kennedy [Pavilion] a tough place to play.

The Kennel Club was ahead of its time.

Joe
Hillock,
Former GU
Assistant & UCLA
Director of Basket-
ball Operations

I have coached college basketball for over 25 years and the old Kennedy Pavilion [Martin Centre] was the loudest building I have ever been in for a college game.

Mark
Few
GU Head
Coach

The Kennel Club not only gives us a great home court advantage, it impacts how recruits who are visiting the GU campus or watching games on TV view our program. Those kids can go to a game of any program in the country and not find a better game environment than what we have at Gonzaga.

Phil
Martelli,
St. Joseph's
Head
Coach

What a tremendous, tremendous atmosphere. And I would have said that even if we had lost the game.

John Calipari, Current Kentucky & Former Memphis Head Coach

Bill Grier, Former GU & Current Colorado Assistant Coach

We know we are going into one of the most hostile places to play anywhere in the country. It's going to be wild. Our biggest challenge may be to keep our focus on what we need to do to be successful, and hopefully, not get distracted by all the stuff happening around us.

When you are on the [Gonzaga] side, [the Zags] walk out of their locker room with a lot of confidence. The students get the rest of the building going. They feed off the energy. It's hard to communicate with your guys. You've got to be really, really tough between the ears to come in here and play with poise.

Steve Alford, UCLA Head Coach

Greg McDermott, Creighton Head Coach

It's an incredible atmosphere. The fans are terrific; [the Kennel Club] is not just energetic the whole game, but they're creative. That's the way student bodies should be.

It's hard to get and keep momentum in a building like this.

Tony Bennett, Current Virginia & Former WSU Head Coach

Randy Bennett Saint Mary's Head Coach

I've been fortunate to coach in a lot of great atmospheres. The Kennel Club ranks up there with some of the best. The combination of the choreographed student section and the high-quality basketball that Gonzaga plays year in and year out makes it a terrific home court advantage.

It's the toughest game on the schedule every year because of [the atmosphere].

WHAT TALKING HEADS SAY

Neil
Everett
ESPN
SportsCenter
Anchor

I'm not a bucket list guy, but I need to break a sweat with those rowdy GU Kennel Clubbers before my time is up. I can feel the heat through the television screen!

Digger
Phelps
Former Notre Dame
Head Coach &
ESPN college
basketball analyst

I've been to (Maryland's) Cole Field House, with the Cameron Crazies at Duke, and the Rock Chalk Jayhawk crew at Allen Fieldhouse, and the Gonzaga Kennel Club ranks up there with the very best.

Dick
Vitale
ESPN college
basketball
analyst

I've been fortunate to call a number of games at McCarthey Athletic Center, and I love the enthusiasm and the passion of the Kennel Club. Spokane is a great place to call a game. It's awesome with a capital A, baby!

Fran
Fraschilla
ESPN college
basketball
analyst

What makes college basketball is the atmosphere in a packed arena. Few have a better or more exciting hoops environment than Gonzaga because of the Kennel Club. The Zags' students are the perfect combination of knowledgeable AND rabid.

Sean Farnham
ESPN college basketball analyst

I love this environment. Do you want to know why college basketball is fantastic? It's because of buildings like this; fan bases like this. They call themselves the Kennel [Club]; they are as passionate as any student body in the country.

Dan Dickau
Pac-12 Network & ROOT Sports college basketball analyst

I am blessed to be able to call games across the west coast and [McCarthey Athletic Center] is the best atmosphere, by far, bar none. But when the students bring it, as they do on the biggest of games, it's not even close.

Tom Hudson
Radio Voice of the Zags

A few minutes before tip-off when the Spartans played at The Kennel in 2011, [Michigan State coach Tom Izzo] walked out of the tunnel and I could see him mouth the word 'Wow' at the sight of the Kennel Club and the atmosphere his team was about to face. After the game (a Draymond Green led 74-67 MSU win), Izzo said he couldn't believe he had brought his team into that environment.

Greg Heister
ROOT Sports Play-by-Play Announcer

I think you can look at the home court record of the Zags during this run, it's one of the most difficult places in the country to play and the Kennel Club is one of the reasons why. I think many teams are beaten before the ball is tipped because of the reputation of the home court advantage.

Right, Coach Mark Few dons the KC shirt while he and Dan Dickau take a postgame interview with ESPN's Jay Bilas.

WHAT THE BOOKS SAY

To be in the Kennel Club means when Eastern Washington fans chanted "Ov-er-ra-ted" at the Zags in 2000, the Gonzaga rowdies responded with "Nev-er rat-ed." To be in the club means that when Loyola managers spread folding stools in a circle during timeouts, you chant "Kum-ba-ya, kum-ba-ya." To be in the club means deciding when to break into the singsong refrain of "It's all ov-er" to symbolize the death of the opponent's chances. Sometimes that can be adapted to the occasion, such as when the Zags led Portland 29-4 in 2001, leading to "Single dig-its" or "Up by twen-ty"—and thirty, and forty, as would be the case in this game.

BraveHearts: The Against-All-Odds Rise
of Gonzaga Basketball
Bud Withers, 2002

The day before the Zags were to meet Minnesota in the first round of their surprise 1999 NCAA Tournament run, the Golden Gophers had to suspend four players for scholastic misdeeds.

One Minnesota official said there was enough "prima facia" evidence of academic misdeeds to warrant the suspension. ("Prima facia" being Latin for: Caught with your pants down.) Apparently, players were having their papers and reports written by a tutor.

It gave the throng of Gonzaga's Kennel Club members invading Seattle's KeyArena plenty of ammo to toss around during the game.

The best sign: "Phlunk the Goferz"

The best chant: "Do your homework... CLAP, CLAP, clap, clap, clap."

Tales from the Gonzaga Hardwood
Dave Boling, 2004

Social Life: This is where Gonzaga excels above most colleges. One of the biggest features the school offers is the Kennel Club, which is a student-run organization that supports the men's basketball team, but also has its own subculture. Almost two-thirds of the student body is part of [the Kennel Club], and social events are almost never missed. This is the cornerstone of the social life at Gonzaga.

The College Buzz Book, 2006

Technically, the McCarthey Athletic Center replaced Kennedy Pavilion (Martin Centre) as the Zags' home court in 2004, but in local parlance, that's when the team moved from The Kennel to the new Kennel. Both arenas have been the headquarters for the rowdy student bunch called the Kennel Club, whose fervor has helped Gonzaga to eight undefeated home campaigns since 1992-93, including a 50-game home win streak from 2002 to '07.

ESPN College Basketball Encyclopedia:
The Complete History of the Men's Game, 2009

WHAT THE POLITICIANS SAY

HOUSE RESOLUTION NO. 2017-4645, by Representatives Riccelli, Shea, Pellicciotti, Holy, Volz, Rodne, Nealey, Ormsby, MacEwen, Steele, Stonier, Sells, Kilduff, Ryu, McCaslin, Kristiansen, Orwall, Chapman, Lovick, Santos, Dolan, Orcutt, Reeves, Gregerson, Johnson, Senn, Slatter, Frame, and Harris

WHEREAS, The Gonzaga University men's basketball team completed the NCAA Division 1 2016-2017 season with 37 victories, a feat only nine teams have accomplished, and advanced to the National Championship matchup against North Carolina; and

WHEREAS, A Pacific Northwest team has not advanced to the championship since 1958; and

WHEREAS, Head Coach Mark Few earned the title of 2017 Naismith and Associated Press Men's College Coach of the Year; and

WHEREAS, Coach Few has led the Zags into the NCAA tournament in each of his 17 years as head coach. Coach Few's other accomplishments include fifteen West Coast Conference titles, five Sweet 16 appearances, two Elite Eight competitions, one Final Four matchup, and a National Championship game; and

WHEREAS, The 2016-2017 Gonzaga men's basketball

team had the best defense in the nation, and won more games and scored more points than any previous Gonzaga team; and

WHEREAS, Gonzaga earned multiple number one rankings, including first in the ESPN Basketball Power Index, as well as a number 1 seed for the NCAA Tournament; and

WHEREAS, Gonzaga University student athletes have the third-highest Graduation Success Rate among all Division I schools in the nation; and

WHEREAS, Gonzaga's Nigel Williams-Goss was selected to the Wooden Award's 10-player All-America team and also received the Elite 90 Award for being the top academic achiever of any player in the Final Four; and

WHEREAS, Gonzaga's Przemek Karnowski finished his career as the NCAA Division I's all-time wins leader with 137, won the Kareem Abdul-Jabbar Award, and made the WCC All-Academic team; and

WHEREAS, Gonzaga has repeatedly committed to a culture of sportsmanship, academic excellence, and dedicated performance on the court; and

WHEREAS, The Zags' reputation as a team of close, resilient, and elite athletes made them a dominating powerhouse all the way to the National Championship game; and

WHEREAS, These extraordinary achievements have been supported by the community of Gonzaga University student body, faculty, staff, alumni, friends, family, benefactors, and fans from throughout the State of Washington; and

WHEREAS, The raucous Kennel Club, Gonzaga's famed student section, has helped the Zags men's basketball team to a record of 177 wins at home, and traveled near and far in large numbers to support their team;

NOW, THEREFORE, BE IT RESOLVED, That the House of Representatives express its thanks and great pride to the players, coaches, staff, and fans of Gonzaga University basketball for their excellence in achievement both on and off the court; and

BE IT FURTHER RESOLVED, That the House of Representatives recognize the value and dedication of student athletes and the excitement and energy of collegiate athletics as a reflection of community pride and support; and
BE IT FURTHER RESOLVED, That copies of this resolution be immediately transmitted by the Chief Clerk of the House of Representatives to the President of Gonzaga University, the Athletic Director of Gonzaga University, the coach of the Gonzaga University Bulldogs men's basketball team, and to each team member.

I hereby certify this to be a true and correct copy of Resolution 4645 adopted by the House of Representatives April 19, 2017

_____

Bernard Dean, Chief Clerk

It is such a distinct honor as an alum to represent Spokane and the district Gonzaga sits in. It was extra special for this former face-painted, chest-lettered Kennel Clubber to formalize our State's pride and appreciation by sponsoring a resolution recognizing the Zags remarkable run to the championship. It's clear the essence of the Kennel Club, that camaraderie, bond and electricity of fandom, brings people together and unifies us in a truly exceptional way.

Marcus Riccelli ('00)
State Representative
Washington's 3rd Legislative District

WHAT THE PRINT MEDIA SAY

"I don't want to take this thing away from the students," says Gonzaga coach Dan Fitzgerald of the on-campus Martin Centre, known locally as The Kennel, where the Bulldogs have won 145 of 183 games under Fitzgerald and where the fans are well prepared to do their part come game time. So for now, Gonzaga will say no to the "downtown people" (as Fitzgerald calls them) who want the Bulldogs to move to the new 12,100-seat Veterans Memorial Arena.

Still, there is much to this home-sweet-home thing. Ninety-four straight non-conference foes over 12 seasons have fallen at Duke: Is it logical to think that the Cameron Crazies had nothing to do with that?

Sports Illustrated, 1995

They're called memories. Biggests and bests, firsts and lasts. This would be a night for the lasts in this building.

The last Blake Stepp hesitation-and-acceleration to the hoop. The last Ronny Turiaf shirt pull and cartoonish grimace. The last alley-oop, the last vestige of Flex, the last "Up by 20!" and "That guy sucks!" from, bless 'em, the Kennel Club.

The Spokesman-Review, 2004
(Blanchette on the last
Martin Centre game)

Throw in the hangar-like arena called The Kennel, the thousands of student members of the Kennel Club who help sell-out its 4,000 seats, and the 12 varsity players who use its secret key-punch code at all hours, and you have the smallest big-time college basketball program in the nation.

The New York Times, 2002

The infamous Kennel Club crowd started working over the Huskies early–an hour before tipoff.

Just two minutes after the doors opened, Gonzaga students, wearing trademark blue T-shirts and standing in the front row, started screaming at [UW's Doug] Wrenn during a team shoot-around. "Hey, Doug!" one guy in particular repeated, over and over, unwilling to quit until he got a response.

"What!" Wrenn finally snapped, ill-advisedly making eye contact.

Before the UW's first set of warmups were over, Kennel Clubbers had commented on everything from the Huskies' uniform color (they wore gold, not purple) to deep sub David Hudson's lack of height (he was referred to as "Gary Coleman").

A half hour before the opening tip, Hudson hit a shot, momentarily silencing his detractors. He then turned and said something snide to the fans as he and his teammates left the floor, drawing a collective roar.

A better comeback would have been a Huskies victory.

Seattle Post-Intelligencer, 2002

"It doesn't get any better than that," Coach Few said of the atmosphere. "I don't care if you're in Cameron Indoor or Allen Fieldhouse ... when you look up and see everyone in red—it's nothing short of amazing. It's inspiring."

Cory Violette chimed in, saying the Kennel Club does everything short of scoring for the Zags: "I think they account for 10 points a game."

The Gonzaga Bulletin, 2003

More than 3,000 students a year join the Kennel Club, a group of supporters who have appeared in ESPN highlight reels and who believe their brand of school spirit (matching red shirts and chanting from seats that are as close to the court as NCAA rules allow) helped Gonzaga earn the third-longest at-home winning streak in college basketball history.

Northwest College Report/ Portland Monthly, 2009

Started by a group of students and Gonzaga baseball players in 1984, the Kennel Club has evolved into a 700-plus member, student-run organization that is a vital part of the Gonzaga basketball experience.

During the dominance of Gonzaga basketball The Kennel was ranked by *Sports Illustrated* at one point as the fourth toughest arena in the country in a survey of opposing teams. Gonzaga's student-run organization is in part responsible for the nightmares other teams have preparing for a trip to play the Zags on their home court.

The Gonzaga Bulletin, 2004

For two hours, a steady chorus of Gonzaga chants was heard, providing an uninterrupted play by play, if not an accurate commentary.

"We've got Heytvelt!"

"Up by 20!"

"Go home, Huskies!"

Zags senior guard Derek Raivio supplied a game-high 25 points, freshman guard Matt Bouldin added a career-high 21 and sophomore center Josh Heytvelt had a workman-like 14 points and 7 rebounds; but the Huskies already knew these guys were highly capable players. It was the supporting cast in the stands that was hard to scout and simulate in practice.

At 9:55 p.m., the game ended and the arena energy level finally tapered off, with the home court win streak never in question. Once again, [the Kennel Club] had done their job.

Seattle Post-Intelligencer, 2006

"This is our house!"

It's one of the Kennel Club's favorite chants, but on Thursday night, the Zags reminded the St. Mary's Gaels that the players believe in that sentiment in a convincing 80-61 win in the McCarthey Center.

The Gonzaga Bulletin, 2010

"When he said, 'Dominum Josephum,' we began to jump around like we were sitting in the Kennel Club section at a Gonzaga basketball game."

The Catholic World Report, 2013
(The reaction in The Vatican's St. Peter's Square upon the announcement of Cardinal Joseph Ratzinger as Pope Benedict XVI)

The first eight minutes had to be Gonzaga's most scintillating in a season that has seen 25 wins. The Zags jumped BYU with seemingly effortless offense, an aggressive man-to-man defense caused 12 misses in the first 16 attempts, and with 12:32 left in the half, Gonzaga led, 23-9.

Kicking up the audacity meter a notch, vacationing students from Gonzaga's Kennel Club chanted, "Why-so-quiet?" at the BYU section across the way.

Seattle Times, 2012
(From the WCC Tournament in Las Vegas)

The power of the Kennel Club is something that has taken on an almost mythical reputation. But perhaps for good reason — the students travel well (including contingents at games as far away as the brutal one-point loss to Butler in Indianapolis in January), can be deafening, and truly feel like they're part of this phenomenon. After they graduate, they come back as the sort of dedicated alumni who continue to bolster the school's athletic programs.

The Inlander, 2013

And just before the second half of [the GU vs. UW] bludgeoning, there they were, the most prescient words of the night scrawled on poster board:

"Only Huskies know how to sit and roll over."

The Olympian, 2017

Twelve-hundred rabid students jumping in unison on mobile bleachers inside McCarthey Athletic Center send pile-driving shocks that reverberate through concrete. Whipped into frenzy before tip-off, the Kennel Club represents the beating heart of a program that has become inextricably linked to Spokane's identity.
"WE. ARE. G-U!"

The Spokesman-Review, 2014

Tipoff was still more than 15 minutes away Friday night and [Creighton's] Marcus Foster couldn't help but smile.

He'd just missed a 3-pointer from the corner during warmups — and the [Kennel Club] standing on the first row of bleachers just about a foot off the sideline were letting him have it. They pointed and screamed.

You typically hear from players in this sport that they find themselves ignoring the crowd — whether those fans are jeering or cheering. But here? Where more than 1,000 students are packed along the length of the floor — and they jump, stomp, yell, clap, chant and sing for several minutes before the game even begins inside a 6,000-seat gymnasium that just seems to amplify the noise?

Yeah, you just have to embrace it.

Omaha World-Herald, 2017

The Gonzaga
Bulletin

Mike Slamkowski
"Luckiest Zag Dad Ever"
Mar 20, 2012

**Observations of a Zag Dad…with thematic quotes from
Coach John Wooden at no additional cost to the reader**

Sports(manship)

After visiting Gonzaga to check on my favorite daughters
and take in a glorious visit to the Kennel for the BYU game, I was
left with the image of a sea of red-shirted Kennel Club members
bobbing to zombie music. The students were rewarded for their
efforts, as the Zags were perfect at home in the WCC this year.
Best laugh of the night was the Kennel cheer to acknowledge
the poor shooting night of guard Matt Carlino of BYU, who was
serenaded with, "You're not Jimmer!" Very clever, and clearly
audible.

If complaints of certain cheers or signs are of poor taste, let's
not get too judgmental about them. A sign stating "What the
Hael is a Gael?" is a clever pun on your fiercest conference rival
and the undergrad who coined it should take a bow ... Let's
keep the PC police from entering McCarthey, even if they have
a press pass.

The Kennel Club is a gem and a privilege to be a part of. So,
enjoy the ride and keep it classy, as you are heard throughout
the campus and the city. The following quote should apply to
the Kennel Club:

"We are many, but are we much?"
John Wooden

146

Student Life

Now in my 50s, I request a "do-over." I attended an Iowa college from 1977-81, when the adult beverage age was 18 (we were mature for our age, back then), but I would be willing to forgo that luxury for a chance to enjoy the 2012 undergrad experience in Spokane. Gonzaga's student body is energetic, compassionate, spiritual, community-minded, resourceful and intelligent. Your Admissions and Financial Aid departments have amassed a gifted group of young adults to attend this top-notch Jesuit university.

It is a parental joy to watch and listen to coeds on campus. Energy and discourse abound in Crosby, competition overflows in Martin Centre intramurals, spiritual reflection exudes at St. Al's and the student chapel, medical facts permeate in the nursing building, team-building is planned at GSBA and University Ministry, military training occurs at ROTC and new Zags meet lifelong friends at C/M, Desmet, Welch and Coughlin. I can only compel all current Zags to pass it on to the Zags that will follow. You are infectious and warm the hearts of your financially strapped parents. We are viewing a core value: your happiness!

"Happiness begins where selfishness ends"
    John Wooden

Faith

I have witnessed many Zags sharing and growing their Jesuit experience. The menu of opportunities to deepen faith includes retreats, ministries, Mass presentation and faith curriculum. The non-Catholic population adds to the diversity and sharing of different faith backgrounds. A student should only need to listen to a returning attendee of a Freshman Retreat or Search retreat to get the urge to sign up for an appropriate weekend for your class level. Failure to attend retreats is a missed personal growth experience, which cannot be recovered upon graduation. Experiencing a weekend may only be eclipsed by helping to put one on.

"If I were ever prosecuted for my religion, I truly hope there would be enough evidence to convict me."
    John Wooden

Approaching the Finish Line, Commencement: May 13, 2012

What has happened between our two generations? The goal of my generation was our senior year rush to graduation, with a career position confidently in hand ... ready to get paid for our own (and our parents') investment in college. Please email me the entire list of May graduates who want to leave Gonzaga. I sense depression on the topic of graduation and leaving this "nest." This is a testament to the relationships you have built during your time here. However, it is time to conquer new fears and challenges. As a parent, I must try and be a resource to the advancement of my two remaining Zag daughters.

How do you students start to let go of the special campus and college life that replaced your preceding fabulous life with your parents? Well, one suggestion is to "shock and awe" your parents by starting a conversation on this topic. If appropriate, you can thank Mom and Dad for past financial and emotional support as you progressed through college. If you have student debt, discuss the options of how it is to be repaid ... if grad school is desired, how can it be funded? If you are not entering full-time employment, how long can a parent possibly carry you on their medical plan (possible until you are 26, for many employers)? Finally, discuss transportation. That car that you may have been driving for a while is likely owned, insured, titled and maintained by a loving and generous parent. Discussing your interest in ownership or full maintenance of the car upon full-time employment may overwhelm your parents with your interest in adulthood.

Talk to your parents ... they may be stunned by your effort! Lower your fear of graduation and life after Gonzaga: It will be a great adventure because you have just completed a priceless educational experience. Your college success is just a start.

"Success is never final; failure is never final. It's courage that counts."
  John Wooden

Reprinted with author's permission

148

DAILY BRUIN

Claire-ification: Gonzaga's Kennel makes UCLA's Den look tame

BY CLAIRE FAHY

Posted: December 12, 2015 11:15 pm

MEN'S BASKETBALL, SPORTS

After camping out the night leading up to the game against UCLA, Gonzaga's student section was in full force an hour before tipoff. (Austin Yu/Daily Bruin senior staff)

f SHARE   🐦 TWEET

Correction: The original version of this article incorrectly stated that there was no camp out for the UCLA vs. Kentucky game on Dec. 3. In fact, there was a camp out.

SPOKANE, Wash. – There are these red T-shirts popular among Gonzaga students that have the words "Official Sixth Man" stamped prominently across the back.

The first time I saw them was walking around campus with my sister during her freshman year in Spokane six years ago.

I didn't get it.

I thought the first guy I saw wearing one was literally the sixth man on the men's basketball team and just happened to be especially proud of himself. My sister had to explain to me that those shirts were in fact given to the entire student section, a group known as "The Kennel."

These supporters are far more than a student section – they really do comprise the team's sixth man. From the sidelines of the McCarthey Center to the Orleans Arena in Las Vegas – home to the WCC Championships – the Kennel provides Gonzaga with a distinct edge.

"They have routines, they do like stunt things, you know I was doing one of the routines one time. That crowd is great and it's fun to play against – it's fun to play with. We get just as hyped when they're going crazy," said senior/forward Tony Parker following Saturday's win. "They were reading my tweets to me and everything. They do their homework – that's a good crowd."

I saw my sister many times on ESPN as she and her friends jumped up and down for the 40-minute game's entirety – a physical feat I can only experience vicariously.

When I arrived at UCLA, I was ready for a similar experience. I knew the storied history of John Wooden and the long list of national championships hoisted by the Bruins. I knew that this was a sports school, full of competitive athletes.

When I arrived on campus, the one thing I found missing was the fan base. Even as an avid basketball follower, I stopped attending Bruin games, uncomfortable in the only ever partially-filled Pauley Pavilion.

Last year I sat down with Bill Walton to discuss his time under Wooden for a feature I was working on. He lamented that the days he knew playing in Pauley were gone – when every seat was filled with an attentive fan ready to see his team take the court.

I tried to camp out for UCLA's 2014 matchup with then-No.1 Arizona – a game that came down to a nail-biting five-point spread – but too many restrictive rules deterred me and many others, rendering the pre-game event unsuccessful. Pauley was packed to the rafters that night, but I was relegated to cheering in the nosebleeds, miles away from my fellow students.

In contrast, hundreds of Gonzaga students were camped out overnight leading up to the UCLA game – braving 30-degree weather and reading textbooks by lamp light. Bruins can't manage that kind of turnout in the perpetual 70-degree temperatures of Los Angeles.

Then again, the Kennel is incomparable in every sense. The McCarthey Center is considerably smaller than Pauley Pavilion. Gonzaga's home court has a capacity of 6,000 compared to UCLA's 12,829. The Kentucky game on Dec. 3 saw the Bruins' largest crowd since 2012 with 12,202. Students arrived less than an hour beforehand and the student section was only filled minutes before the game began. The Kennel arrived in full force over an hour before tipoff on Saturday.

There's an effortlessness to the Kennel's performance. Every student seems to know what to do at every moment, no prompting needed. They all jump and chant and clap in perfect unison without an obvious leader. Over in Westwood, there's an emcee forcing you into an 8-clap or a Bruin spell-out at every timeout.

"It's an incredible atmosphere. The fans are terrific, the student body is not just energetic the whole game, but they're creative," said coach Steve Alford Saturday. "That's the way student bodies should be."

The Kennel reaches an enviable decibel level that had me completely stressed despite the fact I was not the target of the taunts.

"We couldn't really hear each other to be honest with you," said sophomore forward Jonah Bolden.

On the flip side of their fear-inducing function is the school pride infused into every syllable of every rally cry. The student section has you believing that you, too, are "GU", even if you've never attended the school in your life.

While UCLA's 28,000 undergrad enrollment may prevent the student body from having any singular interest, every Gonzaga student believes fervently in this basketball team.

Gonzaga's mascot, Spike the Bulldog, takes a selfie with student supporters during the game. UCLA senior forward/center Tony Parker praised the Kennel's coordination and preparation. (Austin Yu/Daily Bruin senior staff)

Props to the Bruins for finding a way to translate that verbal abuse into fuel for their upset victory. Luckily for UCLA, its sixth man – Jonah Bolden – was on his game Saturday, because the Bruins have no honorary bench players to see them through to victory.

Claire Fahy Sports Editor

|

cfahy@media.ucla.edu

Through the Years:
Kennel Club T-shirts

1984-86

No new shirt was produced for the 1985-86 season.

1986-87*

*Fitz funded new shirts for baseball team. First use of "6th Man."

1987-88†

1988-89

†First sponsored shirt.

1989-90‡

1990-91

‡Design same as 1987-88, but "6th Man" logo omitted from some print runs.

1991-92

1992-93

1993-94¥

1994-95**

¥"Gonzaga" name removed.

**"Gonzaga" name restored.

1995-96*

1996-97

*"Gonzaga" name removed for several years.

1997-98

1998-99†

† University's logo removed entirely.

1999-2000‡

2000-01¥

‡New athletics logo appears.

¥ Note addition of the school year.

2001-02

2002-03

2003-04

2004-05**

** Northern Quest Casino's sponsorship begins.

2005-06

2006-07

2007-08

2008-09

2009-10

2010-11

2011-12

2012-13

2013-14

2014-15

2015-16

2016-17

2017-18

2018-19*

153

The Painted Face Crew, cheering here during a 1984 game, was the core group that later merged with the baseball team to form the Kennel Club.

Through the Years:
Kennel Club Leadership

1987-88	Bob Finn, *First Official KC President*
1988-89	Jason Boyd & Billy Walker, *Co-Presidents*
1989-90	Jim Fitzgerald, *President*
1990-91	Jason Boyd & Steve Brezniak, *Co-Presidents*
1991-92	George Brauer & Dan Greenan, *Co-Presidents*
1992-93	Rich Marzano & John Deasy, *Co-Presidents*
1993-94	Brian Girardot, *President*
1994-95	Damon DeRosa, *President*
1995-96	Tomson Spink, *President*
1996-97	Justin Slack, *President*
1997-98	Justin Slack, *President*
1998-99	Kyle Kupers, *President*
1999-2000	Kyle Kupers, *President*
2000-01	Jeff Billows & Scott O'Brien, *Co-Presidents*
2001-02	Stephen Churney, Sam Shaw & Neil Tocher, *Co-Presidents*
2002-03	Joe Dinges & Jodi Elmose, *Co-Presidents*
2003-04	Jon Love & Mike Wall, *Co-Presidents*
2004-05	Ryan Franklin & Seth Urruty, *Co-Presidents*
2005-06	Matt Skotak & Ian Wehmeyer, *Co-Presidents*
2006-07	Max Malotky & Joe Tomascheski, *Co-Presidents*
2007-08	Chris Haskin & Luke Lavin, *Co-Presidents*
2008-09	Tyler Martin & Kepa Zugazaga, *Co-Presidents*
2009-10	Jack Quigg & A.J. Treleven, *Co-Presidents*
2010-11	Jed Keener & Justin Tai, *Co-Presidents*
2011-12	Kathryn McGoffin, *President*
2012-13	Connor Cahill, *President*
2013-14	Trang Nguyen, *President*
2014-15	Sara Wendland, *President*
2015-16	Sharon Greer, *President*
2016-17	Daniel Incerpi, *President*
2017-18	Claire Murphy, *President*
2018-19	Taylor Woods, *President*

Their impact is evident. Look at our record here.

Mark Few
2017 Naismith Men's College Basketball
& Associated Press Coach of the Year
The Gonzaga Bulletin (2000)

Afterword

Do you want to know the true impact of the Kennel Club? Ask the Gonzaga players and coaches. Ask them the difference between playing a home game when the Kennel Club is in full force versus when the students are on break. Ask the executives at ESPN why Gonzaga is the only school west of the Mississippi to host their *College GameDay* broadcast twice. Ask opposing players and coaches what is the toughest road environment in which they play. Or simply ask anyone who has been to a Gonzaga home game since 1984.

While over the course of those 30+ years some KC chants were less than sympathetic or compassionate toward their intended targets, those instances were relatively few and far between. For the most part, I believe the Kennel Club is an outlet for expressions of creativity and youthful exuberance with an overriding love of the Zags.

The members of the early iterations of the Kennel Club were fortunate in that we were not held to a particular standard; it was the Wild West in terms of any code of conduct, and what little boy doesn't want to be a cowboy? I know I did.

What I have loved most about the KC is its spontaneity. Without youthful spontaneity, would I have jumped out on the Kennedy Pavilion floor with my brother Tim during that timeout in the Whitworth game in 1984? And if we hadn't done that, would Fitz have taken notice and called me to meet with him? Would we have thrown that party and painted our faces? Would the series of events that resulted in the Kennel Club ever have been set in motion? I truly don't know.

Don't get me wrong. Given the astonishing accomplishments of the GU basketball program, I think it's safe to assume that the student body would be very supportive and highly engaged at games, but would the Kennel Club have evolved into what it is today? I doubt it.

The Kennel Club would not have come into existence after the Zags' 13-14 season in 1982-83 or survived the 8-20 season in 1989-90 without students who were willing to paint their bodies, dress up in all sorts of ridiculous outfits and, generally speaking, make fools out of themselves. You have to have a little "Look at me!" in you to continually do those things while your team is regularly getting beat—that is what Coach Ed Goorjian was referring to when he said, "I wish we had guys like you at LMU" (the Lions were 11-16 that season).

> # I TELL YOU WHAT, [opposing] coaches and players like to pretend they're tough. They like to say the Kennel Club doesn't matter, that it has no effect on how they play here. That's bullcrap. They make a difference.
>
> ## Dan Fitzgerald
> *Former Men's Basketball Head Coach and Athletic Director*
> The Inlander *(1994)*

The Kennel Club of today has different challenges: The rules of engagement have changed, but the boundaries-testing mindset of the average college-age person has not. In many ways, I believe I learned more from the consequences of stepping over the line than I would have if someone had constantly kept me in check. Perhaps this is an opportunity lost.

The Kennel Club has a long and illustrious history. Like any successful endeavor, it is a challenge to maintain success and continue to innovate. Being creative and spontaneous while bringing it every night, regardless of opponent, with the class one expects of a group associated with a great University and basketball team is not easy. But what accomplishment of any note is?

By the same token, the University might loosen the reins on the KC to allow them to be more creative and spontaneous. A good place to start would be to reinstate the Kennel Club's use of a specified timeout at each game. Let the KC membership decide how to evolve the timeout. Maybe they'd include the old spell-out, but maybe they'd devise entirely new routines and bring even greater energy to the Kennel. Second, allow the KC to do what it once did best: conduct intel on the opposing team to highlight "fair game" items (as Jack Quigg put it) via chants and signs.

I think those who are concerned about what today's Kennel Club might do with their newfound freedom will be surprised by how responsible young people can be when given the authority that comes with the free expression of thought.

> # I MISS THE LAWLESSNESS
> ## of the Kennel Club of my era, but I still enjoy coming to the games and witnessing the energy the KC brings to the Zags of today.
>
> ## Derek Raivio
> *WCC Co-Player of the Year* (2007)

The KC co-founders are proud that a small group of die-hard Zag fans created something that has grown to be an integral part of "The Gonzaga Experience" for tens of thousands of GU students. And, yes, we are proud that the University has acknowledged the impact of the Kennel Club by emblazoning the name we created and the brand we fostered on the floors of the Martin Centre and the McCarthey Athletic Center. We hope that the powers that be will consider taking it one step further and retire the #6 (which, by NCAA regulations, cannot otherwise be used) to honor the generations of GU students who changed the environment at Gonzaga basketball games forever.

Do you want to know the true impact of the Kennel Club? Ask a Gonzaga graduate from any of the last three decades what they remember most about their time at GU, and I bet one of the first things they mention is the KC.

That's the true impact of the Kennel Club.

Go Zags!

Mike Shields ('84)

GRATITUDE

John Blanchette has been a reporter and columnist for the
The Spokesman-Review and *Spokane Chronicle* for more
than 35 years. John was the first person we approached
when we decided that the Kennel Club's story needed
to be told. To be honest, Aaron and I were hoping he
would write this book for us! Still, John provided us with
much-needed guidance and feedback on our early
writing efforts. John was the perfect person to write our
Foreword. He covered the Zags during the John Stockton
era and was witness to the formation and growth of
the Kennel Club. John's involvement gave this project
credibility it would have lacked without him. Thank you,
John.

Jeffrey Dodd is an Assistant Professor of English at
Gonzaga. Jeff's patient guidance and expertise in literary
design made it possible to complete this book on an
otherwise impossible timeline. Thank you, Jeff.

Bob Finn ('88) is the Alumni Outreach & Engagement
Director at Gonzaga and the first KC President. He played
on the GU baseball team, bartended at Jack & Dan's,
and has worked at GU for nearly 20 years. Bob's contacts
at GU and in Spokane are unparalleled. When we had a
question about a GU alum, Bob was our go-to guy. Thank
you, Bob.

Dale Goodwin ('86) is the Communications Manager/
Senior Writer & Editor at Gonzaga. Dale was a guiding

force on this project from start to finish. He played the roles of editor, fact-checker, photographer, mentor, counselor and friend. His even-handed nature and Zag wisdom helped us navigate the political waters. This project would have been impossible to complete without him. Thank you, Dale.

Mike Harrington, JD, MBA ('84, '91, '92) is Senior Corporate Counsel at Esterline Technologies. Mike is a KCOG and former President of the Knights of Gonzaga (1981-82). He was also a founder and first Commodore of the Gonzaga crew program. Mike and I helped launch the first-ever Gonzaga alumni chapter in Tacoma. He put his GU law degree to good use in providing pro bono legal assistance and advice on this project. Thank you, Mike.

Phil Haugen, Jennifer Mitchell, Julie Holland, Bob Castle, and Jake Patterson ('08) from the Kalispel Tribe and the Northern Quest Resort & Casino who have been tremendous supporters of this project and proud sponsors of the Kennel Club since the 2004-2005 season. Simply put, this book does not come to fruition without their generous support. Thank you, Phil, Jennifer, Julie, Bob and Jake.

Libby Kamrowksi ('18) and **Rob Curley** of *The Spokesman-Review* offered invaluable assistance in locating and accessing photographs – which we hope makes the story come alive more! Special thanks also to **Dan Beach** ('88) for assisting us with this effort. Thank you Libby, Rob, and Dan.

Stephanie Plowman is the Special Collections Librarian at Gonzaga University. Stephanie not only provided us with access to the Gonzaga archives, she spent hours assisting us in locating and securing use of dozens of photos and articles. She was especially helpful in confirming the accuracy of the KC shirt gallery. Thank you, Stephanie.

Dave Soto ('12) is a coach and Sports Information Director at Cate School in Carpinteria, California. He is former Vice President of the KC Board and graduated from GU with a degree in Broadcast Communications and a minor in Journalism. Dave's educational background, his attention to detail and his love of the Zags, made him ideally suited to be our copy editor. He also recruited **Jordan Caskey** to put his production talents to work in helping us with promotional content. Thank you, Dave and Jordan.

SPECIAL THANKS

Frankie Adil-Garcia ('18)
Tim Andress ('96)
Erich Bacher/
    University of Virginia
Caroline Barlow ('01)
Scott Bauer ('87)
Dan Beach ('88)
Zack Berlat ('11)
Jon Bolling ('84)
Jason Boyd ('91)
Andrew Brajcich ('03)
George Brayer ('93)
Steve Brezniak ('91)
Jeff Brown ('94)
Greg Bui ('88)
Tony & Ashley Byrne
Collin Calhoon ('18)
Casey Calvary ('01)
Jordan Caskey
Steve Churney ('02)
Jeff Condill ('86)
Corner Booth Productions
Dominick Curalli ('01)
Rob Curley
Keith Currie
Damon DeRosa ('95)
Ken Devones ('77)
Chris Dooley
Eric "Big Ed" Edelstein ('00)
Rhett Ennis ('01)

The Family of Dan Fitzgerald
Jim Fitzgerald ('92)
Bob Flanagan/ESPN
Richard Fox ('04)
Jackson Frank ('20)
Ryan Franklin ('05)
Robby Furth ('07)
Brian Gabert ('87)
Kathleen Gardipee ('87)
Tucker Gibbons
Brian Girardot ('94)
Marie Girardot ('84)
Gonzaga University
Dylan Graff ('18)
Lauren Grant
Dan Greenan ('92)
Mark Gross/ESPN
Deanne Gustin ('87)
Chris Haskin ('08)
Megan Hawley
Barrett Henderson
Andy Hill
Denise Hill
Jay Hillock ('71)
Joe Hillock ('82)
Sean Hogan ('84)
Eric Johnson/KOMO-TV
Libby Kamrowski ('18)
Jerid Keefer
Jed Keener ('11)

Kyle Kupers ('01)
James Lebeau ('92)
Michael Letts ('18)
Dr. Peggy Sue Loroz ('95)
Sean Lynch ('87)
Kevin MacDonald
Elena Maes
Nick Maiorana/Miami Heat
Kevin Malone ('78)
Rich Marzano ('93)
Chris McGahan ('87)
Kathryn (McGoffin) Lee ('12)
Ted McGregor, Jr./*The Inlander*
Jim McPhee ('90)
Joey Micheletti ('10)
Robert Micheletti ('77)
Warren Miller/Colorado Rockies
Karen Moyer/
    The Moyer Foundation
Claire Murphy ('18)
Avery Myers ('21)
Krissy Myers/Indiana Pacers
John Naekel ('00)
Scott O'Brien ('02)
Breanne ('07) & Shamus
    O'Doherty ('07, '10)
Anna Negron/ESPN
Andy Patton ('13)
Richard "Digger" Phelps
Shawn Phelps ('96)
Chris Pouley ('94)
Jack Quigg ('10)
Derek Raivio ('07)
Krista Rammelsburg ('04)
John Raschko ('12)
Ross Rettenmier ('79)
Marcus Riccelli ('00)
Keli Riley
John Rillie ('95)
Tali Rinaldi

Tony & Karen Rinaldi
Joe Roberts ('84)
Steve Robinson ('78)
Colin Romer/Portland Trailblazers
Mary Roney ('84)
Sam Shaw ('02)
Andy Shields ('96)
Charlie Shields ('18)
Chuck & Dolores Shields
Emily Shields ('21)
Jack Shields
Tim Shields ('87)
Enoch Simmons
Justin Slack ('98)
Andrew Sorenson ('08)
Tomson Spink ('96)
Chris Spring ('87)
Chris Standiford ('91, '93)
Kyle & Dolly Stanley
Sonja Steele
Nate Steilen ('91)
John ('84) & Nada Stockton ('84)
Stacey Stockton
Jeff Sweat
Dr. Ed Taylor ('82)
The Spokesman-Review
MiKealy Thomas ('19)
Neil Tocher ('02)
Joe Tomascheski ('07)
Sara Topf ('02)/Colorado Rockies
Bob Twiss ('84)
Seth Urruty ('05)
Ben Van Houten/Seattle Mariners
Charlie Vogelheim ('78)
Paul Vogelheim ('77)
Mark Walatka ('84)
Billy Walker ('89)
Mike Wallblom
Jeff Zenier ('88)
Kepa Zugazaga ('09)

AUTHORS' NOTE

In the course of writing this book we conducted dozens of interviews, including contact with nearly every one of the Kennel Club Presidents and Co-Presidents from each of the last four decades. While we attempted to include as many stories as possible, limited space and a short time-line precluded us from detailing every story we were told.

Before we stated something as fact or directly quoted someone, we cross-checked that fact or gave the person attributed with the quote the opportunity to review and approve it. Having said that, errors occur and memories fade. While we may not have gotten every detail correct, it wasn't from a lack of effort. We hope that you enjoy this book with the knowledge that we made every attempt to get it right.

Aaron Hill ('01, '02) & Mike Shields ('84)

NOTES AND PHOTO CREDITS

Front cover: Photo by Mike Wootton, courtesy of Gonzaga University Athletics.

Dedication: photo courtesy of Gonzaga University Archives & Special Collections – Foley Library; Monson quote from "Former GU coach Fitzgerald dies" by John Blanchette, *The Spokesman-Review*, January 20, 2010.

Frontispiece: photo courtesy of Gonzaga University Archives & Special Collections – Foley Library.

Page 6: Ted Kennedy photo courtesy of Gonzaga University Archives & Special Collections – Foley Library; Martin Centre sign photo courtesy of Gonzaga University Archives & Special Collections – Foley Library.

Page 7: Adrian Buoncristiani photo courtesy of Gonzaga University Archives & Special Collections – Foley Library.

Page 8: Captain Zag photos courtesy of Gonzaga University Archives & Special Collections – Foley Library; WCC logo courtesy of Gonzaga University Athletics.

Pages 10-16: Photos courtesy of Scott Bauer.

Page 18: Kennedy Pavilion photo and Vanilla Fudge ad courtesy of Gonzaga University Archives & Special Collections – Foley Library; Snake Pit T-shirt photo courtesy of Charlie Vogelheim; Sister Antonia Stare photo courtesy of *The Spokesman-Review* obituary, December 30, 2012; Original Kennel Club T-shirt photo by Tucker Gibbons, courtesy of Mike Shields.

Page 19: Epigraph from "Gonzaga men's hoops: Bulldogs moving out of Kennel" by Bud Withers, *Seattle Times*, February 28, 2004.

Page 21: Nilson quote, personal correspondence with Mike Shields.

Page 23: Hillock quote from "Kennel Club kindles craziness" *The Gonzaga Bulletin*, January 31, 1985; Ed Goorjian photo courtesy of University Archives, Department of Archives and Special Collections, William H. Hannon Library, Loyola Marymount University.

Page 24: Epigraph from "The Edge: Whether it's nerve-racking noise or architectural ploys, some home courts have a built-in advantage" by Jack McCallum, *Sports Illustrated*, October 24, 1995

Page 26: "Kennel Club kindles craziness" *The Gonzaga Bulletin*, January 31, 1985, courtesy of Gonzaga University Archives & Special Collections – Foley Library.

Page 27: Epigraph from "Out of the Kennel," by Paul Seebeck, *The Inlander*, February 9, 1994.

Page 28: Pecarovich Field photo courtesy of Gonzaga University Archives & Special Collections – Foley Library; Hill Crew tank top photo courtesy of Steve Brezniak; Hill Crew photo courtesy of Jeff Condill; 1988 baseball staff photo courtesy of Chris Spring; Rah seat, jacket, and shoes photos courtesy of Chris McGahan; Photo of no-ref night courtesy of Scott Bauer.

Page 29: KC photo courtesy of Scott Bauer; Baseball staff photo courtesy of Gonzaga University Archives & Special Collections – Foley Library.

Page 32: Jay Hillock courtesy of Historic Images; Hillock look-alike photo reproduced with permission from *The Spokesman-Review*, January 19, 1986.

Page 33: 1985 baseball team photo courtesy of Gonzaga University Archives & Special Collections – Foley Library.

Page 34: Blanchette quote from "Gonzaga puts clunker in the rear-view mirror" by John Blanchette, *The Spokesman Review*, December 18, 2017.

Page 35: "Kennel Club solicits membership" from Gonzaga Bulletin, November 21, 1985. Courtesy of Gonzaga University Archives & Special Collections – Foley Library.

Page 36: Epigraph from "Kennel Club takes a rare breed" by John Blanchette, *The Spokesman-Review*, January 31, 1987.

Page 38: "Kennel Club takes a rare breed" from *The Spokeman-Review*, January 31, 1987, reprinted with permission; first sponsored shirt photos courtesy of Mike Shields; Kennel Club women photo courtesy of Caroline Barlow.

Page 39: "Kennel Club takes a rare breed" from *The Spokeman-Review*, January 31, 1987, reprinted with permission.

Page 40: Photo courtesy of Scott Bauer.

Page 41: Epigraph, personal correspondence with Mike Shields.

Page 42: "Kennel Club gives Support to 'Dogs" *The Gonzaga Bulletin*, February 6, 1986, courtesy of Gonzaga University Archives & Special Collections – Foley Library.

Page 43: Epigraph, personal correspondence with Mike Shields.

Page 45: Epigraph, personal correspondence with Mike Shields.

Page 47: Fitz look-alike photo courtesy of Deanne Gustin; Fr. Tony Lehmann photo by Steven Watts, courtesy of Gonzaga University Athletics; Father Tony chair courtesy of Gonzaga University Archives & Special Collections – Foley Library; Fr. Tony in car photo courtesy of Jeff Condill.

Page 48: Photos and scoring list courtesy of Gonzaga University Athletics.

Page 49. Logo courtesy of Gonzaga University Athletics.

Page 50: Epigraph, Brian Girardot, personal correspondence with Aaron Hill.

Page 52: Jeff Brown quote, personal correspondence with Aaron Hill.

Page 53: John Rillie quote, personal correspondence with Aaron Hill.

Page 56: Epigraph, "Encore, Encore! GU Returns to NCAA Tournament" by Steve Bergum, *The Spokesman-Review*, March 7, 2000.

Page 58: Dan Dickau quote from an interview on *The Mark Few Show*, 2017.

Page 60: Photo courtesy of Gonzaga University Athletics.

Page 61: Dench game photo courtesy of Gonzaga University Athletics; Dench wookie photo courtesy of Axel Dench; Tunnel photo courtesy of Gonzaga University Athletics/Explosive Illusions; Crosby photo courtesy of Gonzaga University Athletics; Elvis costumes photo by Allen Hubbard, courtesy of Gonzaga University Athletics.

Page 62: Epigraph from Eric Edelstein, personal correspondence with Aaron Hill.

Page 64: Epigraph: *Signum* was the Gonzaga alumni magazine before it was renamed *Gonzaga Magazine*.

Page 65: Quote from "Out of the Kennel," by Paul Seebeck, *The Inlander*, February 9, 1994.

Page 68: Epigraph from "25 years of getting crazy in the Kennel" by Peter Zysk, *The Gonzaga Bulletin*, October 15, 2008.

Page 70: Lindsay quote from "25 years of getting crazy in the Kennel" by Peter Zysk, *The Gonzaga Bulletin*, October 15, 2008.

Page 71: Inset excerpt from "Chants embarrass Gonzaga" by David Lindsay and Aaron Hill. *The Gonzaga Bulletin*, February 8, 2006.

Page 74: UW 1W-7L Sign photo courtesy of Gonzaga University Archives & Special Collections – Foley Library; "Same Team" ad still shot courtesy of Corner Booth Productions; David Lindsay photo courtesy of Gonzaga University Archives & Special Collections – Foley Library; Bronze Bulldog photo courtesy of Steve Robinson.

Page 75: Epigraph from personal correspondence with Mike Shields.

Page 77: Pendergraft quote personal correspondence with Mike Shields.

Page 81: Photo courtesy of Gonzaga University Archives & Special Collections – Foley Library.

Page 82: Epigraph from "From ball boy to power forward" by Kathryn Zielony, *The Gonzaga Bulletin*, November 10, 2004.

Page 85: Dentmon quote from "'Kennel Club' plays its part for Zags" by Dan Raley, *Seattle Post-Intelligencer*, December 10, 2006.

Page 87: Photo by Allen Hubbard, courtesy of Gonzaga University Athletics.

Page 88: Tent city photo by Young Kwak, courtesy of *The Inlander,* March 7, 2013; tent number distribution photo by Libby Kamrowski, courtesy of *The Gonzaga Bulletin*; *College GameDay* photos courtesy of Gonzaga University Athletics; Adam Morrison photo courtesy of *The Spokesman-Review*.

Page 92: Photo courtesy of Gonzaga University Athletics.

Page 97: Photo courtesy of Gonzaga University Archives & Special Collections – Foley Library.

Page 98: Proposal photos courtesy of Shamus and Breanne O'Doherty; Samhan photos courtesy of Gonzaga University Athletics/Explosive Illusions; KC yelling at Brandon Wiley photo courtesy of *The Spokeman-Review*; Kennel Club entrance photo courtesy of Gonzaga University Athletics.

Page 99-100: Epigraph and display quote from "Saint Mary's College basketball star Omar Samhan not popular among Gonzaga fans" by Jonathan Okanes, *East Bay Times*, February 10, 2010.

Page 101: Photo courtesy of Gonzaga University Athletics.

Page 102: Epigraph from personal correspondence with Mike Shields.

Page 108: Photo courtesy of Gonzaga University Athletics.

Page 109: Epigraph from *The Mark Few Show*.

Page 112: Photo courtesy of Gonzaga University Archives & Special Collections – Foley Library.

Page 113: Sorenson and Hart photos courtesy of Gonzaga University Athletics; Bob Finn and Jack Beach photo courtesy of Dan Beach; Emily and Charlie Shields photo courtesy of Mike Shields.

Page 116: Photo courtesy of Gonzaga University Athletics.

Page 117: Epigraph from personal correspondence with Mike Shields.

Page 121: Top photo courtesy of Dale Goodwin; middle photo courtesy of Mike Shields; bottom photo by Zack Berlat.

Page 123: Epigraph from "Alumni Embrace Zag Basketball" by Meghan Haggerty, *The Gonzaga Bulletin*, March 16, 2005.

Page 124: Photo courtesy of Gonzaga University Archives & Special Collections – Foley Library.

Page 125: Epigraph from personal correspondence with Mike Shields. "Named" Student Support Groups: *Undergrad population - *U.S. News & World Report*, 2017. Note: The University of Kansas, whose student section is consistently ranked among the best in college basketball, does not have a "named" student group. KU has 19,262 undergraduate students.* Sources:
1. Illinipride.com (About Orange Krush)
2. goduke.com (Cameron Crazies)
3. Wikipedia (Izzone; History)
4. Gainsville.com ("Dome sweet home" – 12/16/05)
5. theshowsdsu.com (Show Lore)
6. 225.pitt.edu ("Oakland Zoo!!! What?? We can't hear you")
7. onwisconsin.uwalumni.com (Tradition/The Grateful Red)
8. uknow.uky.edu ("Sharing the Spirit: UK Alum Reflects on Being First

Student EVER in eRUPPtion Zone")
9. zonazoo.wixsite.com (History of ZonaZoo)
10. cyclones.com (Cyclone Alley breaks membership record" – 1/18/07)
11. hoocrew.org (About)
12. Wikipedia (Utah State Aggies; The Hurd)
13. Wikipedia (Crimson Guard (basketball); History)
14. iowahawksnest.org (About)
15. azcentral.com ("Meet the people behind ASU's Curtain of Distraction" – 3/2/15)

Page 126: Photo courtesy of Gonzaga University Athletics.

Page 127: Stockton photo by Keith Currie, courtesy of Gonzaga University Athletics, quote from personal correspondence with Mike Shields; Bryce McPhee photo by Keith Currie, courtesy of Gonzaga University Athletics, quote from personal correspondence with Mike Shields; Condill photo courtesy of Jeff Condill, quote from personal correspondence with Mike Shields; Jim McPhee photo courtesy of Jim McPhee, quote from personal correspondence with Mike Shields.

Page 128: Goss photo courtesy of Gonzaga University Athletics, quote from GoZags.com, 2004; Brown photo courtesy of Gonzaga University Athletics, quote from personal correspondence with Aaron Hill; Rillie photo courtesy of Gonzaga University Athletics, quote from personal correspondence with Aaron Hill; Santangelo photo courtesy of Gonzaga University Athletics, quote from personal correspondence with Mike Shields; Frahm photo courtesy of Gonzaga University Athletics, quote from personal correspondence with Aaron Hill; Nilson photo courtesy of Gonzaga University Athletics, quote from personal correspondence with Mike Shields.

Page 129: Calvary photo courtesy of Gonzaga University Athletics, quote from personal correspondence with Aaron Hill; Dickau photo courtesy of Gonzaga University Athletics, quote from personal correspondence with Mike Shields; Brooks photo courtesy of Gonzaga University Athletics, quote from GoZags.com, 2004; Fox photo courtesy of Gonzaga University Athletics, quote from personal correspondence with Mike Shields; Turiaf photo courtesy of Gonzaga University Athletics, quote from *Seattle Post-Intelligencer*, 2004; Raivio photo courtesy of Gonzaga University Athletics, quote from personal correspondence with Mike Shields.

Page 130: Batista photo courtesy of Gonzaga University Athletics, quote from Senior Night speech; Pendergraft photo courtesy of Gonzaga University Athletics, quote from personal correspondence with Mike Shields; Bouldin photo courtesy of Gonzaga University Athletics, quote from personal correspondence with Mike Shields; Olynyk photo courtesy of Gonzaga University Athletics; David Stockton photo courtesy of Gonzaga University Athletics, quote from personal correspondence with Mike Shields; Wesley photo courtesy of Gonzaga University Athletics, quote from *The Spokesman-Review*, 2014.

Page 131: Sabonis photo courtesy of Gonzaga University Athletics, quote from personal correspondence with Mike Shields; Wiltjer photo courtesy of Gonzaga University Athletics, quote from TheW.tv, 2015; Collins photo courtesy of Gonzaga University Athletics, quote from personal correspondence with Mike Shields; Karnowksi photo courtesy of Gonzaga University Athletics, quote from GU Bulldog Blog, 2013; Perkins photo courtesy of Gonzaga University Athletics, quote from personal correspondence with Mike Shields; Beach photo courtesy of Gonzaga University Athletics, quote from personal correspondence with Mike Shields.

Page 132: Kispert photo courtesy of Gonzaga University Athletics, quote from ROOT Sports/*The Mark Few Show*, February 5, 2018; Melson photo courtesy of Gonzaga University Athletics, quote from personal correspondence with Mike Shields; Williams photo courtesy of Gonzaga University Athletics, quote from ROOT Sports/*The Mark Few Show*, November 28, 2017; Tillie photo courtesy of Gonzaga University Athletics, quote from GoZags.com, April 11, 2018; Richie Frahm running through the tunnel photo courtesy of Gonzaga University Archives & Special Collections – Foley Library.

Page 133: Coaching staff photo courtesy of Gonzaga University Archives & Special Collections – Foley Library; Jay Hillock photo by Keith Currie, courtesy of Gonzaga University Archives & Special Collections – Foley Library, quote from personal correspondence with Mike Shlelds; Joe Hillock photo by Keith Currie, courtesy of Gonzaga University Athletics, quote from personal correspondence with Mike Shields; Few photo by Robert Beck, courtesy of Gonzaga University Athletics, quote from personal correspondence with Aaron Hill; Martelli photo courtesy of Saint Joseph's University Athletics, quote from *Tulsa World*, 2003.

Page 134: Calipari photo courtesy of Gonzaga University Archives & Special Collections – Foley Library, quote from "Game Day, baby!" by Blaine Ritter, *The Gonzaga Bulletin*, 2009; Grier photo courtesy of Gonzaga University Athletics, quote from *The Spokesman-Review*, 2014; Alford photo courtesy of UCLA Athletics, quote from *The Daily Bruin*, 2015; McDermott photo by Mitchell Layton, quote from *USA Today*, 2017; Tony Bennett photo courtesy of UVA Media Relations, quote from personal correspondence with Mike Shields; Randy Bennett photo courtesy of *The Spokesman-Review*, quote from *The Spokesman-Review*, 2017.

Page 135: Everett photo courtesy of *The Spokesman-Review*, quote from personal correspondence with Mike Shields; Phelps photo courtesy of ESPN, quote from personal correspondence with Mike Shields; Vitale photo courtesy of ESPN, quote from personal correspondence with Mike Shields; Fraschilla photo courtesy of ESPN, quote from personal correspondence with Aaron Hill.

Page 136: Farnham photo courtesy of *The Spokesman-Review*, quote from GU vs. Creighton game broadcast, December 1, 2017; Dickau photo courtesy of Gonzaga University Athletics, quote from GU vs. UIW game broadcast, November 29, 2017; Hudson photo by Allen Hubbard, courtesy of Gonzaga University Athletics, quote from personal correspondence with Mike Shields; Heister photo courtesy of Greg Heister, quote from personal correspondence with Mike Shields; Bilas, Few, Dickau photo by Allen Hubbard, courtesy of Gonzaga University Athletics.

Page 141: Riccelli quote from personal correspondence with Aaron Hill.

Page 146: Mike Slamkowski's letter reprinted with permission of *The Gonzaga Bulletin*/Gonzaga Student Media.

Page 149: "Gonzaga's Kennel makes UCLA's Den look tame" article reprinted with permission of the UCLA *Daily Bruin*. Story by Claire Fahy/*Daily Bruin*; photos by Austin Yu/*Daily Bruin*.

Pages 151-153: All images contributed by owners of Kennel Club shirts and printed with permission.

Page 154: Painted Face Crew photo by Scott Bauer.

Page 157: Mark Few quote from "Kennel Club continues to make life miserable for visitors," *The Gonzaga Bulletin*, February 18, 2000.

Page 158: Fitzgerald quote from "Out of the Kennel," by Paul Seebeck, *The Inlander*, February 9, 1994.

Page 159: Raivio quote from personal correspondence with Mike Shields.

Page 177: Photo courtesy of Scott Bauer.

Page 178: Shields and Stockton photo courtesy of State of Washington Sports Hall of Fame; 1998-1999 men's basketball team photo courtesy of Gonzaga University Athletics; Mike Shields and Aaron Hill photo courtesy of Dale Goodwin.

Back Cover: John Stockton photo courtesy of Gonzaga University Athletics; Marco Gonzales photo courtesy of Ben Van Houten/Seattle Mariners; Mike Redmond photo courtesy of the Colorado Rockies.

ABOUT THE AUTHORS

AARON HILL

Aaron earned both Bachelor ('01) and Master ('02) of Business Administration degrees from Gonzaga University. He held a variety of roles within the Gonzaga Athletics Department beginning as a manager for the men's basketball program as a freshman (1997-98) and worked with the program each of his four undergraduate years, being part of the 1998 NIT, 1999 Elite Eight, and 2000 and 2001 Sweet Sixteen teams.

While his work with the basketball program prevented him from being in the Kennel Club at games, Aaron was, nonetheless, a KC member each of his four years at Gonzaga. During his later years as an undergrad and throughout graduate school, he tended bar at Jack & Dan's Tavern. Aaron also served as a volunteer assistant baseball coach before working in Athletic Marketing & Sponsorship. During his freshman year, while watching Friday Night Sports Extra for highlights of future Zag Colin Floyd, Aaron's answer to a trivia question gave him a nickname that stuck—many in the GU community know Aaron as "Hobus" after former GU player Hugh Hobus, who played a part in the trivia answer.

Aaron earned his doctorate in Business Administration from Oklahoma State University (OSU) in 2010. Following graduation, he served on the faculty of OSU-Tulsa and then at the University of Nevada-Reno. In 2012, Aaron returned to OSU as a faculty member at the Spears School of Business, where he taught and served as the Spears Chair his last three years at the school. Aaron now resides in Gainesville, Florida, where he teaches at the Warrington College of Business at the University of Florida.

MIKE SHIELDS

Mike Shields ('84) earned a Bachelor of Business Administration (Economics) from Gonzaga University. He also worked toward a Master's degree in Athletics Administration at GU. Before leaving graduate school to accept the position of Assistant General Manager and, eventually, General Manager for the Texas Rangers' rookie league team in Butte, Montana, Shields served as an administrative assistant to Steve Hertz and the GU baseball program.

The Shields family has deep roots at Gonzaga. Mike's older sister (Kathryn '82), younger brothers (Tim '87 and Andy '96), and sister-in-law (Jody Nielsen '86) are also GU alumni. In fact, between 1978 and 1996, there was only one year (1990) when there wasn't at least one member of Mike's immediate family (i.e., himself or one of his siblings) who was a student at GU. In addition, Mike's oldest son Charlie is a 2018 graduate of Gonzaga and his daughter Emily is a member of the GU class of 2021. Emily served as a volunteer student manager with the Gonzaga women's basketball program, and both Charlie and Emily were members of the Kennel Club. Shields' youngest son, Jack, is a member of the class of 2021 at the University of Wisconsin in Madison.

Mike met his wife, Katie (Wallblom), while she was in nursing school and he was in graduate school, and while both were working as bartenders at Jack & Dan's Tavern. Mike and Katie were married on September 21, 1991 (which just happened to be the same day that John Stockton was named to the original Olympic Dream Team), at St. Aloysius Catholic Church on the Gonzaga campus. Father Tony Lehmann, SJ, and Father Michael Williams, SJ, concelebrated the wedding Mass.

In addition to his time with minor league affiliates of the Texas Rangers and Oakland Athletics, Mike has held numerous other sports management positions during his 30-year career, including Executive Director of the Tacoma-Pierce County Sports Commission; Athletics Marketing Director at the University of Portland; and Vice President of Corporate Partnerships for the

Tacoma Rainiers (Triple-A affiliate of the Seattle Mariners).

Mike is currently an executive committee member of the State of Washington Sports Hall of Fame, and was formerly the Tacoma representative on the Washington State Olympic Committee as an appointee of former Washington governor and WSOC chair, Albert D. Rosellini.

Mike and Katie live in Gig Harbor, Washington, with their two Labrador retrievers, Cody and Brody.

Left to right: Sean Hogan, Mike Harrington (partially obscured) and Mike Shields. To the far left edge of the picture from the 1983-1984 season is Pat Mulligan, former GU basketball student manager and current assistant men's basketball coach at Seattle University; to Mulligan's left is GU baseball player Pete Winning (pointing), and to the far right (in the plaid jacket) is Chris McGahan. From these modest beginnings, the Kennel Club is now known nationwide and travels the country to support the Zags.

Right, Mike Shields presents John Stockton with his State of Washington Sports Hall of Fame induction plaque at a Gonzaga game in 2009 with the Kennel Club in the background.

Aaron Hill, seated far left was student manager for men's basketball as an undergraduate. Here he's with the 1998-1999 team that made a Cinderella run to the NCAA Tournament's Elite Eight.

Among the many similarities shared in their GU experiences, co-authors Mike Shields and Aaron Hill both served as bartenders at Jack & Dan's, a staple of the Gonzaga Community.